BOOKTALKING AUTHENTIC MULTICULTURAL LITERATURE

Fiction, History and Memoirs for Teens

Sherry York

Professional Development Resources for
K-12 Library Media and Technology Specialists

Library of Congress Cataloging-in-Publication Data

York, Sherry, 1947-
  Booktalking authentic multicultural literature : fiction, history, and memoirs for
teens / Sherry York.
      p. cm.
  Includes bibliographical references and index.
  ISBN-13: 978-1-58683-299-5 (pbk.)
  ISBN-10: 1-58683-299-9 (pbk.)
  1. Book talks--United States. 2. Teenagers--Books and reading--United States.
3. Young adult literature, American--Bibliography. 4. American literature--
Minority authors--Bibliography. 5. Ethnic groups in literature--Bibliography. 6.
Pluralism (Social sciences) in literature--Bibliography. 7. Multicultural educa-
tion--Activity programs. I. Title.
  Z1003.15.Y67 2008
  028.5'5--dc22
                                    2007051423

Cynthia Anderson: Editor
Carol Simpson: Editorial Director
Judi Repman: Consulting Editor

Published by Linworth Publishing, Inc.
3650 Olentangy River Road, Suite 250
Columbus, Ohio 43214

Copyright © 2008 by Linworth Publishing, Inc.

ISBN 13: 978-1-58683-299-5
ISBN 10: 1-58683-299-9

Mixed Sources
Product group from well-managed
forests and other controlled sources
www.fsc.org Cert no. SW-COC-002283
© 1996 Forest Stewardship Council
FSC

5 4 3 2 1

TABLE of CONTENTS

TABLE *of* CONTENTS *continued*

TABLE *of* CONTENTS *continued*

TABLE *of* CONTENTS *continued*

ETHINC GROUP ABBREVIATIONS

AA   African American
AI   American Indian
ArA   Arab American
ChA   Chinese American
CoA   Colombian American
CuA   Cuban American
DA   Dominican American
EuA   European American
EIA   East Indian American
FA   Filipino American
HA   Haitian American
JaA   Japanese American
JeA   Jewish American
KA   Korean American
MA   Mexican American
ME   Mixed Ethnicity
PR   Puerto Rican
VA   Vietnamese American

ABOUT *the* AUTHOR

SHERRY YORK worked as an educator in Texas from 1969 through 1999. During those years she was a teacher, school librarian, reading program supervisor, and public library board member. A long-time reviewer, she has published articles and reviews for several publications including *Library Talk*, *The Book Report*, *Library Media Connection*, *ALAN Review*, *Voice of Youth Advocates* (*VOYA*), and others. York is the author of four Linworth books on multicultural literature for young readers and editor of *Tips and Other Bright Ideas for Secondary School Libraries*, volume 3 and *Tips and Other Bright Ideas for Elementary School Libraries*, volume 3. An advocate of multicultural literature, she has presented programs at library conferences in several states. York is a project editor for Linworth Publishing, assisting librarians and educators in manuscript development. She enjoys serving as a judge for Publishers Marketing Association, reading regional mysteries, and browsing the shelves of public libraries in Texas and New Mexico.

ACKNOWLEDGMENTS

Thanks and love to Marlene Woo-Lun, Cyndee Anderson, and all the other friends that God has sent to guide and help me on my new path of life's journey.

Introduction

Who needs this book?

If you want to make your school, your library, or your classroom a more inclusive, welcoming environment for students, this book is written for you. This book is for

- media specialists,
- librarians, and
- teachers

Media specialists and school librarians can use the contents of this book to

- provide booktalks to students and teachers,
- learn more about cultures other than your own,
- build a culturally inclusive climate in your school, and
- select books to increase cultural diversity in your library.

Librarians in public library settings can use this book as a basis for

- planning programs for teen patrons,
- working with patron reading groups of many ages,
- increasing diversity in your library, and
- learning about many U.S. cultures through literature.

Why should librarians and teachers care about multicultural literature?

For students to succeed in our schools, they must *be in our schools*. Every child regardless of ethnicity needs to feel that school personnel care about their well-being. All students want to be liked and accepted for who they are. Being a teenager is seldom easy, and growing up in modern-day society can be a tough proposition. All students, minority and non-minority, should be *comfortable* in our schools and in our libraries.

Everyone wants to be successful. To be successful in the United States in the twenty-first century, students must perform adequately on standardized tests. Student assessment according to *No Child Left Behind* <www.nclb.gov> requires that high-school students pass tests in order to graduate. Reading and critical thinking are essential skills that high-school students must possess in order to pass mandatory tests.

No Child Left Behind mandates "accountability for results." Scores on standardized tests are reported according to economic background, *race and ethnicity*, and English proficiency and disability. Therefore, educators should realize that cultural understanding is important. Educators have a moral duty to reach *all* teens.

Schools, students, and teachers are being judged by standards and test scores. They are being evaluated by statistics based on drop-out rates, students' performance on standardized tests, and adequate yearly progress. What is the connection between multicultural literature, a love of reading, and student achievement? Common sense tells us that an inclusive environment fosters happy children, good readers, low drop-out rates, and high test scores.

The National Center for Fair & Open Testing <www.fairtest.org> on authentic accountability at <www.fairtest.org/authentic-accountability> addresses student well-being. As our schools and our society become more diverse, we must strive to meet the needs of *all* our students. Authentic multicultural literature can help librarians and teachers provide a welcoming respectful atmosphere for our students and make the school culture more inclusive.

The National Standards for the English Language Arts <www.ncte.org/about/over/standards/110846.htm> were written by the National Council of Teachers of English (NCTE) and the International Reading Association (IRA). Students who read, understand, and enjoy these books of contemporary fiction, memoirs, and multicultural history will be meeting many Language Arts Content Standards. If students write or speak about books they have read, they will be meeting Language Arts Content Standards for writing and speaking for expression. These books can connect students to literature to help them meet standards for literature and cognitive skills. If students want to read more of the works of specific authors, learn about people's lives through memoirs, or learn about the places involved in the stories, memoirs, and histories, then they may develop research skills, another National Language Arts Standard.

The National Standards of the National Council for the Social Studies are found at <www.socialstudies.org/standards>. Since these booktalks are based on books that have connections to United States and global cultures, they meet National Social Studies Standards for understanding cultures and perceptions of places and regions.

Media specialists will likely be familiar with the Information Literacy Standards for Student Learning of the American Library Association (ALA) and the Association for Educational Communications and Technology (AECT). Standards 4, 5, 7, and 9 found at <www.ala.org/ala/aasl/aaslissues/aaslinfolit/informationliteracy1.cfm> relate to students' personal interests, appreciation of literature, diversity of viewpoints, cultural perspectives, and respect for the ideas and backgrounds of others. These attributes can be promoted through multicultural literature.

Educators know that students must be engaged and interested in order to learn. Students who are active learners will be more successful test takers. Students who read and appreciate literature are learning. Multicultural literature in libraries and classrooms can help engage students and enable them to perform to their potential on standardized tests and in the real world.

Library collections need to reflect the ethnic make-up of student populations. Even in the rare areas in which no ethnic minorities attend schools or visit libraries, library collections and classrooms need to include authentic well-written, non-stereotypical books that reflect the diversity of most of our country's population.

Seeking out culturally-authentic books and materials for libraries is not enough, however. Those good books must find their way into the hands of teen readers, and those stories must find their way into teens' minds and hearts. That is a challenge and responsibility for librarians and teachers.

Librarians and teachers will find that the contents of this collection of booktalks can help

- promote cross-cultural understanding in library media centers and classrooms,
- engage students from a variety of cultures through literature,
- provide opportunities to make minority students feel accepted,
- prevent dropouts,
- improve test scores,
- achieve standards,
- make curriculum connections, and
- facilitate collaboration.

What does this book contain?

Part I explains the importance of authentic multicultural literature. It includes a brief discussion of the importance of authenticity, multiculturalism, and diversity.

Part II contains one hundred and one booktalks of books of contemporary fiction, memoirs, and history by ethnic or multicultural authors of the United States. Some of these titles are specifically for young adult or teen readers. Others are for general audiences or adult readers.

Most booktalks include:

Book title

Author: Brief biographical information and current Web address, if available

Publication information: Publisher and date, number of pages

Genre: Contemporary fiction, memoir, or historical fiction

Level: Young Adult or Adult

Note: Relevant book information such as awards received or recommended lists

Summary: Fiction titles include Library of Congress or other equivalent summaries

Subjects: Modified Dewey, Library of Congress, and other subject headings

Read-aloud excerpt: A section of the book that could serve as a booktalk

Booktalk: A sample or starter booktalk for the busy librarian or teacher

Related Titles: Additional books on related themes or by that author

---

Following the booktalks, readers will find a bibliography of resources, a subject index, a title index, and an author index.

What criteria were used to select titles for booktalks?

The booktalks in this book were selected to provide the widest possible sampling of ethnicities and minority groups to offer librarians and teachers choices to meet the needs and interests of all students and patrons. Although other titles by ethnic authors may also have merit, the author chose these titles as a starting place for broadening the perspective of teen readers and to demonstrate that many emotions and situations are universal, regardless of ethnicity or culture.

Contemporary fiction titles may capture the interests of teens and encourage them to realize that many themes transcend culture. Booktalks on memoirs can provide a starting place for readers to learn more about outstanding and interesting members of several multicultural groups. Most memoirs are historical, a history of a life. These personal narratives are, therefore, also a part of multicultural history. Historical fiction titles are included so teen readers will come to understand that there are alternate views of the history of the United States. Indeed each cultural group has its own history in the United States. Often those cultural histories are not included in textbooks.

The books included in this text can provide teens with other perspectives to our multicultural history and society. With the passage of time, more authors of young adult literature represent unique ethnic backgrounds. Not all minorities are represented in the young adult literature published each year. However, there are currently more offerings by ethnic authors in the area of contemporary fiction and historical fiction than ever before.

All one hundred and one booktalks are based on books that are in print at the time this manuscript is being written. Some *related titles* are out of print. The out-of-print titles are included because these books may already be on the shelves of libraries and media centers.

ISBNs were not included. Although all one hundred and one booktalk titles are in print at this time, not all bindings and editions of each title are currently in print. Also, new editions with new ISBNs may come into print in the future.

How can librarians use this book?

Librarians and media specialists can use these booktalks and the accompanying information to add diversity to existing library collections, to learn about the backgrounds of the myriad of cultures that make up our society, to support the school's curriculum with authentic multicultural books, and to increase cultural awareness and an appreciation for the roles that many ethnic groups have played in our multicultural history.

- Book displays
- Web page displays
- Newsletters
- Book reviews
- Podcasts
- Staff development
- Shared reading/reading circles/reading groups and discussions
- Collaboration with teachers

What should booktalkers realize about multicultural literature?

Many of these same rules apply for booktalking any book:

- Always read the book before presenting a booktalk.
- Consider the interests, backgrounds, and maturity levels of the audience.
- Be aware of community standards.
- Understand that by booktalking a title, you are implying your approval and endorsement.
- Be honest about your opinions and biases about the book.
- Reveal your dramatic nature and passion for books and reading.
- Be enthusiastic!

Some cautions may be in order if multicultural literature is new to you. Embrace the differences. Do not shy away from leaving your comfort zone. You have everything to gain if you take a chance and venture into the realm of multicultural literature.

The book itself, the read-aloud excerpt, and the booktalk may contain names, words, and phrases that are foreign to you if you are not familiar with that language or culture. As you prepare to do booktalks, check a dictionary or online source to find the proper pronunciation of unfamiliar terms or names . Be open about the fact that you do not speak or read that other language. Let your audience know that you are open to being corrected if anyone can spot a pronunciation error you have made. Allowing your teen audience to see that none of us speaks all languages can be a valuable lesson. Encouraging input and help from audience members can significantly change the group dynamics in place.

> Regardless of the ethnic make-up of your audience, do not focus on anyone based on their ethnicity or skin tones. Why? Teens in general do not like to be singled out from the group. Teens from other cultures are no different. Calling attention to ethnic differences in the audience will be counterproductive. Promoting an us-versus-them climate is not conducive to diversity. Emphasize that we will all benefit from sharing the points of view of others through literature.

PART I

The Importance of Authenticity, Multiculturalism, and Diversity

W e live in a multicultural society that is becoming increasingly diverse with each passing day. Schools, libraries, and classrooms need to welcome students of all ethnic groups. Drop-out rates among minority students in this country are appalling. We are far from the ideal of universal education for all members of society. We need to build school climates in which **every** student is respected and included.

Authentic multicultural literature is written by a person who is a member of the culture about which she is writing. Authentic multicultural literature is not written by a person of another cultural or ethnic group who *thinks* they know what life is like in another culture.

In the early days of education when a tiny awareness of cultural differences began to emerge, some publishers took the idea of multiculturalism to mean that a book's illustrations should contain an African American and an Asian American. That was easy to accomplish by simply darkening the skin of one character to a brown tone and of another to an olive tone. Some even went the extra mile and changed the hair and eyes of these darker-skinned prototypes. Voila! Instant multiculturalism—not.

Because there were almost no persons of color publishing children's or young adult literature, textbooks and anthologies occasionally contained the writings of non-minority authors who, usually with the best of intentions, included ethnic characters in their writings. Those writers included details taken from what they *thought* they knew about a particular culture.

For example, Mexican Americans were often depicted as poor migrant workers who were illiterate, usually victims, often drunkards or sexually promiscuous. With this stereotypical mindset, books for younger readers usually focused on the downtrodden victims of society trying to achieve a better life against impossible odds. The poor folk made the best of their situations and occasionally a plump mama with hair in a bun wearing a serape cooked up exotic Mexican foods like tortillas and enchiladas for a fiesta in which papa played the guitar and the children danced the Mexican hat dance. Authentic culture? Hardly.

Finally, a handful of gifted minority authors like Pat Mora, Virginia Hamilton, Joseph Bruchac, and a few others wrote through the lens of cultural experience and their works for young readers were published. Then librarians and teachers realized there are other points of view in literature. Non-minority educators began to understand that a culture is made up of more than foods and traditions. Readers of authentic multicultural literature could understand that *surface* culture is superficial, not authentic.

No single author, regardless of skill or scope of experience, can represent an entire cultural group. Each author can only write from within his experiences and his life. When a sufficient number of ethnic authors have published books that reflect slices of life from a cultural background, then readers can begin to appreciate the richness and variety of specific cultures.

For example, if I read the books of Mexican American authors Juan Felipe Herrera and Francisco Jimenez, I learn about migrant workers. If I read Gary Soto's books, I learn about growing up in California. When I read Diane Gonzales Bertrand's books, I begin to understand about the experiences of middle- and working-class Tejanos. As I read Hector Cantu and Carlos Castellanos' *Baldo* comic series, I experience a modern Latino family. Which of these is authentic? All of them.

By reading a variety of authentic Mexican American literature, I eventually come to understand that their culture is multifaceted and complex. Certain commonalities connect members of that cultural group, but their differences are vast. When I understand that basic fact, then I cannot continue to stereotype them. I can no longer think of Mexican Americans as a homogeneous group. That is the power of authentic multicultural literature.

I never enjoyed the history classes that I took during almost two decades in classrooms in schools, colleges, and universities. My grades were adequate because I was a good reader, but my knowledge of history was superficial at best. After I read books by multicultural authors, my attitude toward U.S. history changed. Now the dates and events that I memorized years ago have meaning because I understand that happenings in history are parts of a larger picture, pieces of a giant jigsaw puzzle. History is, in a larger sense, a collection of stories of what happened in individual lives. History books tell only part of the story. The multicultural context is missing.

Reading the works of multicultural authors will help students understand the history of our country. Reading memoirs, contemporary fiction, and historical fiction by multicultural authors will expand students' horizons and make them better students and citizens.

PART II

Booktalks

1. Almost a Woman

Author: **Esmeralda Santiago**, born in Puerto Rico, came to the mainland as a teen. Santiago has worked as a film producer and writer and lives in the state of New York. <www.esmeraldasantiago.com>

Publication: Perseus Books, 1998; Vintage Books, 1999. 336 pages

Genre: Memoir   *Level:* Adult

Note: Alex Award, CineSol (Latino Film Festival) Award

Subjects: New York—Biography, Puerto Ricans—Biography, Santiago, Esmeralda

Read-aloud excerpt: Pages 16 through 18

Booktalk: Esmeralda Santiago came to New York with her mother, brothers, and sisters from Puerto Rico in 1961. When she started school there, Esmeralda did not speak English. She was placed in a class with students who had behavior problems, those who had low intelligence-test scores, and those who were waiting to drop out. Using picture books from the public library, she gradually learned English. When the family moved and Esmeralda transferred to Junior High School 33 for ninth grade, she scored well on a series of tests that showed that she had aptitude. The school counselor arranged for her to apply to Performing Arts High School where she could receive an academic rather than a vocational education. Being singled out for this special consideration earned her ridicule from some family members and jealousy from some of her fellow students. Lulu, one of a tough gang of girls who were already tormenting her, cornered Esmeralda in the restroom and spat in her face, but she was determined to defy her tormenter. She fought back by refusing to cry. With her mother's help and lots of determination, she made it to the all-important audition, the audition that could be her entry into a new life.

Related Titles:
Silent Dancing by Judith Ortiz Cofer. Arte Público Press, 1990
When I Was Puerto Rican by Esmeralda Santiago. Vintage, 1994; Da Capo Press, 2006

2. Always Running: La vida loca, Gang Days in L.A.

Author: **Luis J. Rodriguez**, Mexican American, was born in El Paso, Texas, and grew up in California. After a tumultuous childhood he became a poet and writer, founded Tia Chucha Press, and works as a peace maker in Chicago and California. <www.luisjrodriguez.com>

Publication: Curbstone Press, 1993; Simon & Schuster, 1994, 2005. 260 pages

Genre: Memoir   **Level:** Adult

Note: Carl Sandburg Nonfiction Award, Books for the Teen Age (NYPL)

Note: A Spanish-language version is available.

Subjects: Gangs—Biography, Mexican Americans—Biography, Rodriguez, Luis J., 1954-

Read-aloud excerpt: Pages 136 through 139

Booktalk: This is poet Luis J. Rodriguez's account of his vida loca (crazy life) in Las Lomas barrio of Los Angeles, California. He began writing *Always Running* when he was fifteen and finished it in 1992 as a gift for his son Ramiro, who at age seventeen was another troubled, angry young man. Between the ages of twelve and eighteen, Luis was involved in gangs. By the time they were eleven, he and his friends had recognized that they would have to band together to protect each other and avoid being hurt or killed. Luis went to Garvey Junior High, a nightmare of a school where teachers regularly had nervous breakdowns, where rival gangs and violence reigned. He began to use drugs and alcohol. Violent behavior and crime became a normal part of his life. By the time he was eighteen, Luis felt like, and was, the veteran of a war with post-traumatic stress syndrome. This is Luis's story of his teenage years, but it is also the story of hundreds and thousands of teens of his generation and, sadly, of the next generations, a continuing story of poverty, of prejudice, of the soul-destroying ills that society chooses to ignore.

Related Titles:
Crews: Gang Members Talk to Maria Hinojosa by Maria Hinojosa. Harcourt Brace, 1995
East Side Dreams by Art Rodriguez. Dream House Press, 1999

3. American Born Chinese

Author: **Gene Yang**, Chinese American, started drawing comics in the fifth grade. Producer of several award-winning comic books, Yang is a computer science teacher at a high school in the San Francisco Bay Area. <www.geneyang.com>

Publication: First Second, 2006. 233 pages

Genre: Contemporary fiction   *Level:* Young Adult

Note: A graphic novel. Michael L. Printz Award, Best Book of the Year (*SLJ*)

Summary: The book alternates three interrelated stories about the problems of young Chinese Americans trying to participate in the popular culture and is presented in comic book format.

Subjects: Cartoons and comics, Chinese Americans—Fiction, Identity, Schools—Fiction

Read-aloud excerpt: Pages 23 through 29

Booktalk: If you like comics and humor, you may be interested in this graphic novel, the story of how the son of immigrants adjusts to school life. Jin Wang's parents came from China and met in San Francisco. Jin, American-born, spends his first years with his engineer father and librarian mother in an apartment in Chinatown. His playmates are children much like him. When he is in third grade, his family moves. Now Jin finds that he is different from everyone else, definitely an outsider. Jin's classmates believe that Chinese people eat dogs. Jin becomes the victim of Peter Garbinsky, an oversized bully nicknamed "Peter the Eater" for his habit of picking his nose. When Wei-Chen Sun, a Chinese immigrant boy, enters the class and tries to be friends, Jin refuses his friendship, declaring that he has enough English-speaking friends although he has none. In time, Jin becomes "Danny" and begins to look like the other kids in school. Then Chin-Kee, a buck-toothed, yellow-skinned stereotypical Chinese nightmare of a cousin, shows up to complicate and devastate "Danny's" life.

Related Titles:

China Boy by Gus Lee. Plume, 1994

Homebase: A Novel by Shawn Wong. Plume, 1991

Locas: The Maggie and Hopey Stories by Jaime Hernández. Fantagraphics, 2004

Palomar: The Heartbreak Soup Stories by Gilbert Hernández. Fantagraphics, 2003

4. American Chica: Two Worlds, One Childhood

Author: **Marie Arana**, of mixed heritage, has been involved in book publishing as an editor and vice president. An editor at the *Washington Post*, she has served on the boards of the National Association of Hispanic Journalists and the National Book Critics Circle. Arana lives in Washington, D.C. and Peru. <www.loc.gov/bookfest/2001/arana.html>

Publication: Dial Press, 2001. 309 pages

Genre: Memoir   *Level:* Adult

Subjects: Arana, Marie, Journalists—Biography, Mixed descent—Biography

Read-aloud excerpt: Pages 154 through 155

Booktalk: Marie Arana's father was Peruvian. Her mother was American. Marie's parents met in the United States when her father enrolled as a graduate student at MIT. Her mother was studying the violin. She was older than he, had been married three times before, and chose not to discuss her past. In spite of their vast differences, the two married, had three children, and each in turn struggled to fit into a society that was completely foreign to their experience and cultural backgrounds. Marie's earliest memories set in Peru were of earthquakes, ghosts, aristocratic grandparents, a large house with a veranda, and a Spanish-speaking world. In time, the family moved to the United States where Marie met her cowboy grandfather and a tobacco-chewing cousin, was made fun of because of her poor English, and was spat on by a little girl at her new school. As she matured Marie came to see herself as a hybrid, a Latina and an Anglo, a bridge between two very different cultures.

Related Titles:

A Place in El Paso by Gloria Lopez-Stafford. University of New Mexico Press, 1996

5. Ask Me No Questions

Author: **Marina Budhos**, of mixed descent has a Jewish American mother, and her father is Indo-Guyanese. She teaches English at a university and lives in New Jersey. <www.marinabudhos.com>

Publication: Atheneum Books for Young Readers, 2006. 162 pages

Genre: Contemporary fiction   *Level:* Young Adult

Note: Best Books for Young Adults (ALA)

Summary: Fourteen-year-old Nadira, her sister, and their parents leave Bangladesh for New York City, but the expiration of their visas and the events of September 11, 2001, bring frustration, sorrow, and terror for the whole family.

Subjects: Bangladeshi Americans—Fiction, Family life, High schools—Fiction, Illegal aliens—Fiction, New York—Fiction, Schools—Fiction

Read-aloud excerpt: Pages 29 through 32

Booktalk: Bangladeshi Americans Nadira and Aisha attend Flushing High School in New York. Nadira and her older sister don't get along. Nadira thinks everyone considers her the slow-witted plump sister, a follower. Aisha is the star, the perfect one, quick and smart, on the debate team. She makes good grades and plans to go to college on a scholarship, then to Harvard Medical School to become a doctor. Then the terrorist attacks of September 11 change everything. Their visas have expired and the lawyer hired to do the paperwork for them has disappeared so another lawyer was working on their applications for residency. After the Patriot Act led to a crackdown on Muslims and illegal immigrants, Nadira's family began to hear about people being jailed and businesses raided. Now it seems they are no longer welcome in this country so they decide to drive to Canada and ask for asylum. They hope Canada will let them in. Then perhaps they can open a restaurant and Aisha can attend a university. What happens at the border is the beginning of a nightmare that keeps getting worse and worse.

Related Titles:

An American Brat by Bapsi Sidhwa. Milkweed Editions, 1995

6. Autobiography of My Dead Brother

Author: **Walter Dean Myers**, African American, was born in West Virginia and grew up in Harlem. The author of more than sixty award-winning books, he lives in New Jersey. <www.teenreads.com/authors/au-myers-walterdean.asp>

Publication: HarperTempest/Amistad, 2005. 212 pages

Genre: Contemporary fiction   *Level:* Young Adult

Note: Illustrated by Christopher Myers. Best Books for Young Adults (ALA)

Summary: Jesse uses his sketchbook and comic strips to make sense of his home in Harlem and the loss of a close friendship.

Subjects: African Americans—Fiction, Drive-by shootings, Friendship, Gangs—Fiction

Read-aloud excerpt: Pages 5 through 8

Booktalk: Jesse is an artist, best friend, and blood brother of Rise. They had a ceremony mingling of their blood when Rise was nine and Jesse was seven. Now they often attend funerals of friends, victims of drive-bys and gang violence. Rise was Jesse's hero until Rise's junior year when he started getting in trouble and skipping school. Jesse started to hang with C.J., a nerd but a talented musician. C.J., Jesse, and Rise belong to a black social club called the Counts. Rise starts talking about taking over the Counts, about dealing drugs. Lots of things seem to be going on behind the scenes. Jesse doesn't understand the changes in Rise and doesn't like what he sees happening. Jesse and Rise don't seem to communicate like they used to. Then Jesse starts to sketch and draw cartoons, trying to make sense of what's going on. Rise likes having Jesse draw his biography so Jesse keeps drawing, trying to keep in touch the only way he can. Will it be enough?

Related Titles:
The Afterlife by Gary Soto. Harcourt, 2003

7. Barefoot Heart: Stories of a Migrant Child

Author: **Elva Treviño Hart**, Mexican American, grew up in Texas. As a child she traveled with her family as migrant workers. She earned college degrees in mathematics and computer engineering. After a career in computers, she lives in Virginia.

Publication: Bilingual Press/Editorial Bilingüe, 1999. 237 pages

Genre: Memoir   *Level:* Adult

Note: Violet Crown Book Award, Before Columbus American Book Award, Alex Award

Subjects: Hart, Elva Treviño, Mexican Americans—Biography, Migrant agricultural laborers

Read-aloud excerpt: Pages 44 through 45

Booktalk: Elva Treviño was the youngest of six children. She was a small child when the family first went north to work in the fields of Minnesota. They left behind family and friends in Pearsall, Texas, but few material possessions. They did not own a car or a house. Elva's school-age brothers and sisters had to leave school early, and they were ashamed of the reason they had to leave. In Minnesota, everyone worked except the two youngest children who were taken to a Catholic school where they stayed for months while their mother, father, and older brothers and sisters worked long hard hours in the fields. From Minnesota they went to Wisconsin and then back to Texas for the start of the next school year. Elva's father was a hard worker who spoke no English. He had not been able to go to school himself and he knew the only way to survive was for the whole family to work in the fields. He wanted his children to graduate from high school so year after year the family went north to endure long hours of back-breaking labor for little pay. Year after year they returned to Pearsall's segregated schools so that the children could have a chance at a better future.

Related Titles:

The Caballeros of Ruby, Texas by Cynthia Leal Massey. Panther Creek Press, 2002

Farmworker's Daughter: Growing Up Mexican in America by Rose Castillo Guilbault.
Heyday Books, 2005

Jessie De La Cruz: A Profile of a United Farm Worker by Gary Soto. Persea Books, 2000

Migrant Daughter: Coming of Age as a Mexican American Woman by Frances Esquibel
Tywoniak and Mario T. García. University of California Press, 2000

8. Barrio Boy

Author: Ernesto Galarza, born in Mexico in 1905, came to the United States as a child, earned several college degrees, worked as a labor organizer, was the author of several nonfiction books, and died in 1984.

Publication: University of Notre Dame Press, 1971; Holt, Rinehart and Winston, 2000. 275 pages

Genre: Memoir   **Level:** Adult

Note: Author was nominated for a Nobel Prize in Literature.

Subjects: Galarza, Ernesto, 1905-1984, Mexican Americans—Biography

Read-aloud excerpt: Pages 211 through 213

Booktalk: Ernesto Galarza was born in a village in the mountains of western Mexico in 1905. Events of the Mexican Revolution caused him and his mother to move to several places in Mexico. Eventually they came to Arizona and then settled in Sacramento, California. This memoir is the story of his acculturation, how he learned about life in the United States, the education he received, how he ceased being a Mexican and became a Mexican American. Galarza was one of the first Mexican Americans from a poor background to attend college and earn advanced degrees: a master's degree from Stanford and a doctorate from Colombia University. He worked as a labor organizer and wrote a book, *Merchants of Labor*, in 1964. *Barrio Boy*, a memoir of his early life, was nominated for a Nobel Prize in 1976.

Related Titles:

Dionicio Morales: A Life in Two Cultures by Dionicio Morales. Piñata Books, 1997

Knight Without Armor: Carlos Eduardo Castañeda 1896-1958 by Félix D. Almaráz, Jr.
Texas A&M University Press, 1999

Memorias: A West Texas Life by Salvador Guerrero. Edited by Arnoldo De León. Texas Tech
University Press, 1991

9. Beacon Hill Boys

Author: **Ken Mochizuki**, who grew up in Seattle, Washington, is Japanese American. He is the author of award-winning picture books, fiction, and nonfiction for young readers. <www.eduplace.com/kids/hmr/mtai/mochizuki.html>

Publication: Scholastic Press, 2002. 201 pages

Genre: Contemporary fiction *Level:* Young Adult

Note: Asian/Pacific American Award

Summary: In 1972 in Seattle, a teenager in a Japanese American family struggles for his own identity, along with a group of three friends who share his anger and confusion.

Subjects: Individuality, Japanese Americans—Fiction, Seattle, Washington

Read-aloud excerpt: Pages 1 through 2

Booktalk: Japanese American Dan Inagaki is sixteen years old in 1972. He lives in Seattle, Washington, with his father, mother, and older brother Brad. Brad is the family favorite, a great athlete who makes good grades, will go to the right college, and apparently can do not wrong. Dan, on the other hand, cannot seem to do anything right. His hair is too long. He does not have a job. He is not a good athlete. His father says he needs character. When he works without pay for two weeks at an ice cream parlor, gets a haircut at his new boss's insistence, and finally quits when he sees that the man is using him as free labor, his father is furious. At school Dan is friends with Jerry Ito, Frank Ishimoto, and Eddie Kanegae, who call themselves the "Beacon Hill boys." At school Dan wishes he could talk to the beautiful superstar student Janet Ishino, experiences feelings of inadequacy as a sports team member who never gets to play, and resents the racism he encounters. When his friends turn to marijuana and other drugs to deal with the despair they experience daily, Dan decides to take another path.

Related Titles:

One Thousand and One Cranes by Naomi Hirahara. Delacorte, 2008

10. Behind the Eyes

Author: **Francisco X. Stork**, born in Mexico, came with his parents to the United States when he was nine. An attorney and the author of several books of fiction, Stork lives in Massachusetts. <www.franciscostork.com>

Publication: Dutton, 2006. 246 pages

Genre: Contemporary fiction *Level:* Young Adult

Note: Américas Award, commended title

Summary: Sixteen-year-old Hector is the hope of his family, but he seeks revenge after his brother's gang-related death and is sent to a reform school.

Subjects: Family life—Fiction, Gangs—Fiction, Interpersonal relations, Mexican Americans—Fiction, Reformatories, San Antonio, Texas, Self-realization

Read-aloud excerpt: Pages 17 through 19

Booktalk: Sixteen-year-old Hector Robles has spent years trying to make sure that no one notices him. A smart kid, he likes to read, does well in school, and had started reading the *Bhagavad-Gita* when the trouble started. A guy named Chava is head of the Discipulos, one of the gangs that run things in El Paso. Hector's brother Filiberto falls in love with Gloria, Chava'a girlfriend. Fili wants to make things right but winds up dead in a game of chicken when his truck stalls on the railroad track. Hector goes a little crazy when he sees Gloria with Chava soon after his brother's death. Hector attacks the gang leader, is beaten to a pulp, hospitalized, and misses his brother's funeral. Then Chava puts a marker out on Hector's life.

Related Titles:

Woman Soldier, la Soldadera by Irene Beltran Hernandez. Blue Rose Books, 1998

11. Behind the Mountains

Author: **Edwidge Danticat**, who began life in Port-au-Prince, Haiti, was raised by an aunt and uncle in Haiti until at age twelve, she joined her parents in Brooklyn. Danticat is the author of several award-winning books of fiction.
<http://reach.ucf.edu/~aml3930/danticat/>

Publication: Orchard Books 2002. 166 pages.

Genre: Contemporary fiction   *Level:* Young Adult

Note: First Person Fiction series. Américas Award Honorable Mention

Summary: Writing in the notebook her teacher gave her, thirteen-year-old Celiane describes life in Haiti and her experiences in Brooklyn after the family immigrates.

Subjects: Diaries, Emigration and immigration, Haiti, Haitian Americans—Fiction, Immigrants—Fiction, New York—Fiction

Read-aloud excerpt: Pages 1 through 5

Booktalk: Celiane receives a little book with blank pages from her teacher for having the best grades in her class for the past month. On October 18, 2000, she begins to write in her journal. The first entries are about her life in the mountain village of Beau Jour in Haiti. Celiane writes about her father who is living and working in the United States, her mother with whom she lives, her brother Moy, and her friend

Thérèse. In late October she writes about the family's upcoming trip to the city to visit Tante Rose. The time of the presidential elections is approaching. Celiane soon realizes that the political situation, candidates, and parties are much more important here in the city than in Beau Jour. Celiane's mother has not been feeling well so their visit is extended for a few days for medical tests and to allow time for her to rest and gain strength. When Celiane and her mother do start the long trip back to their home, something totally unexpected happens to alter their lives and the lives of all their family.

Related Titles:
Before We Were Free by Julia Alvarez. Knopf, 2002

12. Bigmama Didn't Shop at Woolworth's

Author: **Sunny Nash**, African American, is a photographer, television producer, and writer. She lives in southern California.
<www.tamu.edu/upress/BOOKS/1996/nash.htm>

Publication: Texas A&M University Press, 1996. 186 pages

Genre: Memoir   *Level:* Adult

Subjects: African Americans—Biography, Nash, Sunny, 1949-, Segregation, Texas—Biography

Read-aloud excerpt: Pages 17 through 20

Booktalk: Sunny Nash grew up in Candy Hill, the African American section of segregated Bryan, Texas, in the 1950s. When she was four, Sunny attended her first movie. She and her mother dressed in their Sunday clothes and walked along the rocky graveled streets of their part of town until they reached a nicer neighborhood with pavement, sidewalks, and fine houses with lawns. On Main Street where they stopped at a café for a burger, Sunny and her mother had to go to the back door of the café. Sunny couldn't have a drink because there wouldn't be a restroom for her to use. The cook took their order after waiting on the white people first, insisted on being paid before he prepared their food, and brusquely told them they could not eat inside the café. They ate standing outside. At the theater they stood in the rain outside the ticket window while white moviegoers bought their tickets inside the lobby. Rain soaked, they entered the theater through the back stairs and sat in shabby worn seats in an unlit balcony. Sunny soon came to understand the strengths of her mother, grandmother, family and friends who endured the ugliness of prejudice and segregation.

Related Titles:
Dreams from My Father by Barack Obama. Three Rivers, 2004; Crown, 2007
The Heart of a Woman by Maya Angelou. Random House, 1987; Bantam, 1997
Pride of Family by Carole Ione. Harlem Moon, 2004

13. Birdland

Author: **Tracy Mack** is Jewish and a native of New York. An editor, she lives in Brooklyn and the Berkshires.
<http://content.scholastic.com/browse/contributor.jsp?id=1093>

Publication: Scholastic Press, 2003. 198 pages.

Genre: Contemporary fiction   *Level:* Young Adult

Summary: Fourteen-year-old, tongue-tied Jed spends Christmas break working on a school project filming a documentary about his neighborhood, where he is continually reminded of his older brother, Zeke, a promising poet who died the year before.

Subjects: Brothers, Jews—Fiction, New York—Fiction, Speech disorders, Video recordings

Read-aloud excerpt: Pages 10 through 12

Booktalk: Jed and his friend Flyer set out to make a film documentary about their New York neighborhood as a requirement for a class they are taking. It's the Christmas holidays and Jed's Jewish family does not celebrate that holiday. Jed's older brother Zeke died not long ago. His mother and father are not helping him deal with that situation. Jed has developed a speech impediment. His friend Flyer has his own problems since his parents split and his mom moved to another state. Flyer leaves with his dad to visit relatives, Jed finds Zeke's notebook of poetry, meets a homeless girl with haunting eyes, and searches for the truth.

Related Titles:
Goy Crazy: A Novel by Melissa Schorr. Hyperion, 2006

14. Blessed by Thunder: Memoir of a Cuban Girlhood

Author: **Flor Fernandez Barrios**, born in Cuba, was fourteen in 1970 when she came to the U.S. She makes her home in Seattle.

Publication: Seal Press, 1999. 244 pages

Genre: Memoir   *Level:* Adult

Subjects: Cuban Americans—Biography, Fernandez Barrios, Flor

Read-aloud excerpt: Pages 13 through 16

Booktalk: I am Flor Fernandez Barrios. I was born in Cuba and was a year old in 1956 when Fidel and Raúl Castro and Che Guevara came to the island and went into hiding while they prepared to start a revolution. Almost everyone hated Batista, who had been dictator since the 1930s, but my father, who said that Castro made too many promises, was arrested by the Batista government police because he *might* be for the revolutionaries. During Castro's takeover many people were killed, some because it was *suspected* that they did not like Castro. My grandparents lost their farm after the communists took over. Soon there were shortages of almost everything. In 1965 it was announced that Cubans who wanted to leave the island could. We filed our papers and then waited, waited, and waited. I remember the day I took home a letter from school that said my classmates and I would be sent to the "countryside" to "camp out" with our teachers. We would work in the tobacco and sugar cane fields for forty-five days. I was barely ten years old, had never been separated from my parents, knew nothing about field work, and was very afraid. What would I do?

Related Titles:
Scattering the Ashes by María del Carmen Boza. Bilingual Press/Editorial Bilingüe, 1998

15. Bloodlines: Odyssey of a Native Daughter

Author: **Janet Campbell Hale**, a Coeur d'Alene artist and a writer, was born in California. Hale has taught at colleges and universities and lives in Idaho. <www.nativewiki.org/Janet_Campbell_Hale>

Publication: Random House, 1993; HarperPerennial, 1994; University of Arizona Press, 1998. 187 pages

Genre: Memoir   *Level:* Adult

Note: American Book Award

Subjects: Coeur d'Alene women—Biography, Hale, Janet Campbell, Indians of North America—Biography

Read-aloud excerpt: Pages xviii through xxi

Booktalk: Janet Campbell Hale's childhood was not happy. Alcoholism and domestic violence made her parents' marriage a troubled one. Janet's mother was verbally and emotionally abusive toward Janet, her youngest daughter. The mother and daughter moved frequently causing Janet to change schools often. In this memoir she writes about her Coeur d'Alene and Irish ancestry, about being an American Indian, about her family history, about her people's history, and about her struggles to find her path to become a writer.

Related Titles:
Bead on an Anthill by Delphine Red Shirt. University of Nebraska Press, 1998
Completing the Circle by Virginia Driving Hawk Sneve. University of Nebraska Press, 1995
Te Ata: Chickasaw Storyteller, American Treasure by Richard Green. University of
    Oklahoma Press, 2002

16. Blue Jasmine

Author: **Kashmira Sheth** moved to the United States from India as a teenager.
Blue Jasmin is her first book. Sheth lives in Madison, Wisconsin.
<http://kashmirasheth.typepad.com>

Publication: Hyperion Books for Children, 2004. 186 pages.

Genre: Contemporary fiction   *Level:* Young Adult

Note: Paul Zindel First Novel Award

Summary: When twelve-year-old Seema moves to Iowa City, she leaves friends and family behind in her native India but gradually begins to feel at home in her new country.

Subjects: East Indian Americans—Fiction, Family life—Fiction, Immigrants—Fiction, India, Interpersonal relations, Iowa City, Iowa

Read-aloud excerpt: Pages 137 through 139

Booktalk: Seema Trivedi is twelve when her parents decide that they will leave India to live in Iowa City in the United States. Seema's father is a microbiologist who loves his work. Once before, he had left his family in India while he worked for months in the U.S., but this time his family will go with him. Leaving behind her grandparents, aunt and uncle, and cousins who have always been a part of her life is very hard. Seema's first experiences in Iowa are difficult because the climate is very strange, her English is so poor she is embarrassed to speak, she has no friends, and everything is different. Things begin to look a bit better when she meets Jennifer and Ria and they become friends. Her new teacher is kind and she starts attending an English as a Second Language (ESL) class. Her life at school continues to improve until a new student, Carrie Schuler, moves in from Chicago and begins to lead a make-fun-of-Seema campaign, writing nasty notes about her and mocking her. Finally after Seema has had enough, she finds the courage to fight back.

Related Titles:
Koyal Dark, Mango Sweet by Kashmira Sheth. Hyperion, 2006

17. Born Confused

Author: **Tanuja Desai Hidier**, South Asian American, has worked as a magazine editor, filmmaker, songwriter, and a singer in a rock band and now lives in England. <www.thisistanuja.com>

Publication: Scholastic Press, 2002. 413 pages

Genre: Contemporary fiction   *Level:* Young Adult

Note: Best Books for Young Adult (ALA), BCCB Blue Ribbon

Summary: Seventeen-year-old Dimple discovers that she is not Indian enough for the Indians and not American enough for the Americans, as she sees her beautiful, manipulative best friend taking possession of both her heritage and the boy she likes.

Subjects: Best friends, East Indian Americans—Fiction, Friendship, Identity, Photography—Fiction

Read-aloud excerpt: Pages 9 through 11

Booktalk: Dimple Lala is an ABCD, an American Born Confused Desi, an Indian American. Her parents are from India, and Dimple often feels that she is caught in the middle, between cultures. It seems she is either too much or not enough—too Indian to suit Americans and too American to suit her family. During the confusing summer of her seventeenth birthday, the only things that keep Dimple going are her photography and her long-time friend Gwyn. Then her mother's old friend comes for a visit and brings along her son Karsh. He is an okay guy, just so suitable it is embarrassing. Her parents are thrilled, but Dimple is not. Later Dimple sees Karsh again at a club where he is a talented DJ and she begins to rethink her first impression of him. Meanwhile, Gwyn decides that she and Karsh are destined to be together. Now Dimple is really confused. Will she have to choose between Gwyn and Karsh? Does she have a choice? Is it already too late?

Related Titles:

Motiba's Tattoos by Mira Kamdar. Plume, 2000

What I Meant— by Marie Lamba. Random House, 2007

18. Bowman's Store: A Journey to Myself

Author: **Joseph Bruchac**, of Abenaki Indian and Slovak ancestry, has earned many awards for his numerous books and a lifetime achievement award from the Native Writers' Circle. He lives in Greenfield Center, New York. <www.josephbruchac.com>

Publication: Dial Books, 1997; Lee & Low Books, 2001. 315 pages

Genre: Memoir   *Level:* Young Adult

Note: Paterson Prize

Subjects: Abenaki Indians—Biography, Bruchac, Joseph, 1942-, Indians of North America—Biography, Mixed descent—Biography, New York—Biography

Read-aloud excerpt: Pages 190 through 194

Booktalk: The subtitle of this memoir by Joseph Bruchac is *A Journey to Myself.* Sonny Bruchac grew up at Bowman's Store in Greenfield Center, New York. Sonny lived with his grandparents and never spent a night in his parents' home although they lived nearby. His father was a troubled, angry man who physically and emotionally abused Sonny while his mother did nothing to protect her son. His grandparents provided the stability and love that he desperately needed. His grandfather was Abenaki Indian but called himself "French." From his grandfather Sonny learned about the natural world, trees and animals. His grandmother was overly protective of her grandson who was often the target of bullies because he wore glasses, was always ready to tell on those kids who picked on him, ran away from fights, and was inevitably the last to be picked for any sports team. By the time he became a teenager, Sonny began to understand that his own behavior had led to his lack of friends. In high school he found a way to be accepted by the other kids and became successful in life.

Related Titles:
The Dream Bearer by Walter Dean Myers. HarperCollins, 2003

19. Breaking Through

Author: **Francisco Jiménez**, Mexican American, emigrated to the U.S. from Mexico as a child. The author of a number of award-winning books, Jiménez is a professor at Santa Clara University in California. <www.scu.edu/fjimenez>

Publication: Houghton Mifflin, 2001. 199 pages

Genre: Fiction/Memoir   *Level:* Young Adult

Note: Américas Award Winner, Pura Belpré Honor, Tomás Rivera Award Winner

Note: A Spanish-language version is available.

Summary: Fourteen-year-old Francisco works in the fields and fights to improve his life and complete his education.

Subjects: Agricultural laborers, California—Fiction, Illegal aliens, Mexican Americans—Biography, Mexican Americans—Biography, Mexican Americans—Fiction

Read-aloud excerpt: Pages 1 through 4

Booktalk: Francisco Jiménez left El Rancho Blanco in Jalisco, Mexico, when he was four years old. He, his mother, his father, and his older brother Roberto went to California where they all worked in the fields and lived in migrant labor camps until Francisco was fourteen. Then his brother got a year-round job as a janitor at an elementary school so that the family could live in one place. During those ten years, Francisco had lived with the ever-present fear that he would be seized by the Border Patrol and sent back to Mexico because he and some of his family had entered this country illegally by crawling under a tall wire fence on the California-Mexico border. Francisco loved school and knew that his only chance to get an education was in the United States because the village in Mexico he had left ten years earlier did not have a school at all. On the day that he and his classmates had memorized the preamble to the Declaration of Independence to recite in their social studies class, his worst fears were realized. The Border Patrol came to Miss Ehlis's classroom and took him away.

Related Titles:
The Circuit by Francisco Jiménez. University of New Mexico Press, 1997
La Linea by Ann Jaramillo. Roaring Brook Press, 2006
Small-Town Browny/Cosecha de la Vida by Simón Silva. Arte Cachanilla, 1998

20. Bronx Masquerade

Author: **Nikki Grimes**, African American poet and the author of several award-winning books, was born and raised in New York City and lives in California. <www.nikkigrimes.com>

Publication: Dial Books, 2002. 167 pages

Genre: Contemporary fiction   *Level:* Young Adult

Note: Coretta Scott King Award Winner

Summary: While studying the Harlem Renaissance, students at a Bronx high school read aloud poems they've written, revealing their innermost thoughts and fears to classmates.

Subjects: African Americans—Fiction, Ethnicity, High schools—Fiction, New York—Fiction, Poetry, Schools—Fiction

Read-aloud excerpt: Pages 3 through 4

Booktalk: Wesley is notorious for not turning in homework. His friend Tyrone has seen so many drive-bys he lives only for the moment because he doesn't believe he has a future. Chankara goes to school with a bruised face behind sunglasses. Raul is an artist and so is Diondra, but everybody thinks she should play basketball because she is so tall. Devon has the height and skills to play ball but he would rather go to the library and read. Lupe thinks maybe she would like to have a baby because Gloria's baby is so cute. Raynard is dyslexic. Judianne, Tanisha, Amy, Sheila, Steve, and others in Mr. Ward's English class seem to have absolutely nothing in common until they each find the courage to read their poems during Open Mike Fridays.

Related Titles:
Harlem Hustle by Janet McDonald. Farrar, Straus and Giroux, 2006
Jazmin's Notebook by Nikki Grimes. Dial Books, 1998

21. Bucking the Sarge

Author: **Christopher Paul Curtis**, African American, grew up in Michigan, is a graduate of the University of Michigan, worked at an auto assembly plant for thirteen years, writes full-time, and lives in Ontario, Canada. <www.randomhouse.com/features/christopherpaulcurtis/>

Publication: Wendy Lamb Books, 2004. 259 pages

Genre: Contemporary fiction   *Level:* Young Adult

Note: Best Books for Young Adult (ALA), Best Book of the Year (*SLJ*), Parents' Choice

Summary: Deeply involved in his manipulative mother's shady business dealings, fourteen-year-old Luther keeps a sense of humor while running the Happy Neighbor Group Home For Men and dreaming of going to college and becoming a philosopher.

Subjects: African Americans—Fiction, Flint, Michigan, Mothers and sons—Fiction, People with mental disabilities

Read-aloud excerpt: Pages 29 through 31

Booktalk: Luther T. Farrell's ambition in life is to win the science fair for three years in a row at Whittier Middle School. Although he is only fourteen, he has a driver's license and drives an eighty thousand dollar vehicle. In his wallet he carries three credit cards, a library card, and fifty dollars [and a condom so old it belongs in a museum]. He is six feet four and weighs maybe 135 pounds. His goatee consists of six individual hairs.

Luther's mother, Sarge, is a hard-as-nails business woman who makes money as a loan shark and operator of group homes. Luther works like a man, or a slave, taking care of a group of elderly men who live in a group home. He does not receive a salary, but Sarge makes deposits in a college account for him. The account contains over ninety thousand dollars. Luther plans to study philosophy and become the world's best-known philosopher, but Sarge wants him to join her in the business when he gets out of school. When Luther's science fair project exposes some of his mother's evil practices, Sarge is furious and gives him an ultimatum: pack up and get out or face the consequences.

Related Titles:
Miracle's Boys by Jacqueline Woodson. G. P. Putnam's Sons, 2000

22. Burro Genius

Author: **Victor Villaseñor**, Mexican American author of a number of award-winning books, was a dyslexic high-school dropout. A public speaker and a spokesperson for cultural diversity, he lives in California. <www.victorvillasenor.com>

Publication: Rayo, 2004. 321 pages

Genre: Memoir   *Level:* Adult

Subjects: Authors, American—Biography, California—Biography, Mexican Americans—Biography, Villaseñor, Victor

Read-aloud excerpt: Pages 91 through 94

Booktalk: School was a nightmare for Victor Villaseñor from the very first day of kindergarten when he started to school at age five. He was unable to speak English because his parents spoke only Spanish in their home on a ranch in California. When he asked to go to the bathroom, he was scolded for speaking Spanish. He wet his pants and had to spend the rest of the day in urine-soaked clothes. One of his Spanish-speaking classmates was slapped repeatedly, called a spic, and had his mouth washed out with soap. That was Victor's first day of school. Soon he began to have nightmares and to wet the bed. When the time came to learn to read, things did not improve because Victor was dyslexic. He had to repeat the third grade twice because he could not read. After years of dealing with unsympathetic, bigoted, and sadistic teachers, Victor reached the point where he fantasized about killing one of his teachers. This memoir is an account of how a little Mexican American boy from a ranch in California overcame incredible odds to become a widely-known author and public speaker.

Related Titles:
Rain of Gold by Victor Villaseñor. Arte Público Press, 1991
Thirteen Senses by Victor Villaseñor. Rayo, 2001
Walking Stars by Victor Villaseñor. Piñata Books, 1994

23. Call Me Henri

Author: **Lorraine M. López,** Mexican American, is a California native. An author, editor, and a professor at Vanderbilt University, she lives in Tennessee. <www.vanderbilt.edu/english/lorraine_lopez>

Publication: Curbstone Press, 2006. 237 pages

Genre: Contemporary fiction   *Level:* Young Adult

Summary: Faced with family problems, difficulty in school, and gangs in the barrio, Enrique dreams of some day reaching the "other America" depicted on television, while sympathetic teachers support his fight to study French instead of English as a Second Language (ESL).

Subjects: California—Fiction, Family life—Fiction, French language, Gangs— Fiction, Mexican Americans—Fiction, Middle schools, Schools—Fiction

Read-aloud excerpt: Pages 1 through 4

Booktalk: At Peralta Middle School, Enrique Suarez is in ESL class again. He does not think he needs English as a Second Language for another year and would like to take French instead, but no one, teachers, principal, or counselor, is willing to help him. At home, things are not good either. His mother and stepfather both work, so after school Enrique is responsible for taking care of the triplets, his three baby brothers. His stepfather has a drinking problem, but even when he is not drinking, he does not like his stepson and often hits Enrique when he is angry. One day Enrique stops to play basketball after school. Suddenly he realizes he will be late if he does not hurry home so he cuts through gang territory to save time. That is when Itchy jumps him.

Related Titles:
Jesse by Gary Soto. Harcourt Brace, 1994
Roll Over, Big Toben by Victor M. Sandoval. Piñata Books, 2003

24. Confessions of a Closet Catholic

Author: **Sarah Darer Littman** is Jewish. She worked as a financial analyst before becoming a writer. She has been a newspaper columnist and lives in Connecticut with her children. <www.sarahdarerlittman.com>

Publication: Dutton Children's Books, 2005; Puffin Books, 2006. 193 pages

Genre: Contemporary fiction   *Level:* Young Adult

Note: Sydney Taylor Award Winner

Summary: To be like her best friend, Justine decides to give up Judaism, but after her grandmother dies, she realizes that she needs to seek her own way of being Jewish.

Subjects: Catholics—Fiction, Conduct of life, Family life—Fiction, Grandmothers, Identity, Jews—Fiction, New York—Fiction, Religions

Read-aloud excerpt: Pages 3 through 6

Booktalk: Justine is Jewish by birth, but she does not really understand what it means to "be Jewish." Her father's mother keeps a kosher kitchen, but her other grandparents eat shrimp and lobster that the Torah says should not be eaten. Justine's parents go to the synagogue for special holy days about twice a year. Justine decides she will pick her own religion so she studies Islam, Hinduism, and Buddhism, but they all have serious drawbacks like the possibility of being reincarnated as a cockroach or having to fast all day for a month. Justine envies her friend Mary Catherine's Catholic family and decides to become Catholic. Her first step is to give up being Jewish for Lent, but she does not have the nerve to tell her parents. She also has given up meat for Lent, which makes eating their traditional Friday night Shabbat dinner a real problem since almost every dish is chicken in one form or another. She practices taking communion and confessing her sins in the closet of her room as she prepares to convert, but she soon discovers that religious conversion is more complicated than she expected.

Related Titles:

Pink Slippers, Bat Mitzvah Blues by Ferida Wolff. Jewish Publication Society, 1989

25. Copper Sun

Author: **Sharon Draper**, an African-American writer, teacher, and conference speaker, has won a number of Coretta Scott King Awards for her novels. She lives in Cincinnati. <www.sharondraper.com>

Publication: Atheneum, 2006. 306 pages

Genre: Historical fiction   *Level:* Young Adult

Note: Coretta Scott King Award Winner

Summary: A slave and an indentured servant escape a Carolina plantation to make their way to Fort Moses, Florida, a Spanish colony that gives sanctuary to slaves.

Subjects: African Americans—Fiction, Florida—Fiction, Slavery—Fiction, South Carolina

Read-aloud excerpt: Pages 69 through 71

Booktalk: Amari was fifteen and engaged to be married when strangers came to the African village of Ziavi where Amari's people had lived in peace and harmony for generations. Although the strange white-skinned visitors were unlike anyone the villagers had seen before, good manners dictated that they show hospitality and prepare a welcoming ceremony. After food and drink were shared and stories told, the dancing and drumming began. Then, shockingly, the killing started. One after another of the villagers were shot, stabbed, brutally killed. Soon Amari's parents and her little brother lay dead. Their homes burned as the captives were led away in shackles and chains. Amari and other strong young people from the village were soon to be packed like freight onto a ship bound for the Carolinas to be sold as slaves. Amari wanted to die, hoped to die during the journey but survived to be sold at auction, a birthday present for a plantation owner's sixteen-year-old son.

Related Titles:
Middle Passage by Charles Johnson. Atheneum, 1990
Which Way Freedom? by Joyce Hansen. Walker, 1986

26. Crashboomlove: A Novel in Verse

Author: **Juan Felipe Herrera**, a Mexican American poet and the author of several picture books, novels, and books of poetry, teaches Chicano studies at California State University in Fresno. <www.creativewriting.ucr.edu/people/herrera>

Publication: University of New Mexico Press, 1999. 155 pages

Genre: Contemporary fiction   *Level:* Young Adult

Note: Américas Award Winner

Summary: After his father leaves, César García lives with his mother and struggles through painful experiences of growing up as a Mexican American high school student.

Subjects: High schools—Fiction, Mexican Americans—Fiction, Schools—Fiction

Read-aloud excerpt: Pages 26 through 28

Booktalk: Sixteen-year-old César García lives with his mother Lucy in Fowlerville, California. His dad has another life now in Denver with another wife and other kids. Trouble seems to follow César as he finds himself in situations that he cannot escape. A new kid challenges him to a fight after school. What else can he do? Then he has to support his friends in the fight between the Mexicans and Hmongs. He and his friends sniff glue in the restroom and markers in the classroom until finally César is caught and suspended. Things are a little better at Sunway Continuation, a school for students who have been kicked out of other schools, until the time they smoked a little weed, borrowed a car, and then tragedy struck.

Related Titles:
Downtown Boy by Juan Felipe Herrera. Scholastic, 2005

27. Cuba 15

Author: **Nancy Osa** is a native of Chicago, Illinois, whose father is Cuban. She now lives in Portland, Oregon. *Cuba 15* is Osa's first novel. <www.nancyosa.com>

Publication: Delacorte Press, 2003. 277 pages

Genre: Contemporary fiction   *Level:* Young Adult

Note: Américas Award Honorable Mention, Pura Belpré Honor 2004

Summary: Violet Paz, a high school student, reluctantly prepares for her upcoming "quince," celebration of a Cuban-American girl's fifteenth birthday.

Subjects: Chicago, Illinois, Cuban Americans—Fiction, High Schools—Fiction, Quinceañera (Social custom)

Read-aloud excerpt: Pages 1 through 3

Booktalk: Violet Paz is intrigued when her grandmother wants to provide a quinceañera for her during the year of her fifteenth birthday until she learns that she will have to wear a dress. Violet does not wear dresses, ever! She does realize that this celebration of her crossing the threshold to womanhood will mean a great deal to her Cuban grandparents and maybe even her father although he never has much to say about their Cuban heritage. Violet goes along with the idea reluctantly at first. Her mother and father and then her friends get involved in the planning and what started out as a small idea keeps growing and growing.

Related Titles:

Quinceañera Means Sweet 15 by Veronica Chambers. Hyperion, 2001
Sweet Fifteen by Diane Gonzales Bertrand. Piñata Books, 1995

28. Cubanita

Author: **Gaby Triana** was born in Miami, Florida. Her parents are Cuban immigrants. Triana has been a teacher and is the author of several novels for young adults. <www.gabytriana.com>

Publication: HarperCollins Pub., 2005. 195 pages

Genre: Contemporary fiction   *Level:* Young Adult

Summary: Isabel, eager to leave Miami to attend the University of Michigan and escape her overprotective Cuban mother, learns about her family's past and makes important decisions about the type of person she wants to be.

Subjects: Cuban Americans—Fiction, Identity, Interpersonal relations, Miami, Florida, Mothers and daughters—Fiction

Read-aloud excerpt: Pages 1 through 3

Booktalk: Isabel Díaz just graduated from high school. In August she will be leaving Miami to go to the University of Michigan. Meanwhile, she has a job teaching art at a summer camp in Everglades National Park. She just broke up with Robi because she wanted to start college with her life as free of complications as possible. Another complication is her mother who is Cubanita, a woman who has remained closely connected to her Cuban roots although it has been many years since she left Cuba. Isabel was born in this country, considers herself an American, and does not really understand her mother's lingering connection to Cuba which is, after all, a communist country. Her mother does not mind interfering in Isabel's life in any and all ways. After Isabel meets Andrew Corbin, a coach at the camp, her life gets even more complicated with her mother right there in the middle of the whole mess.

Related Titles:
It's Not About the Accent by Caridad Ferrer. MTV Books, 2007

29. Dandelion Through the Crack: The Sato Family Quest for the American Dream

Author: **Kiyo Sato**, Japanese American, was born in California. She was moved to a "relocation camp" during World War II, served in the United States Air Force, and is a public health nurse. <www.dandelionthroughthecrack.com/pages/author.html>

Publication: Willow Valley Press, 2007. 397 pages

Genre: Memoir   *Level:* Adult

Subjects: Arizona, California—Biography, California—History, Japanese Americans—Biography, Poston Relocation Center, World War, 1939-1945

Read-aloud excerpt: Pages 106 through 109

Booktalk: My name is Kiyo Sato. My parents were Japanese immigrants, but I was born in this country. On December 8, 1941, I was a student at Sacramento Junior College. That Monday morning as I walked through the halls, I realized something was wrong. Students were avoiding me. One person refused to return my greeting, turning away as though she had not heard me. Why? On Sunday, Japan had bombed Pearl Harbor. That began our reign of terror. My father, mother, eight brothers and sisters, and I ceased being Americans. We became Japs, the enemy, suspected spies. Because of President Roosevelt's Executive Order 9066, our rights disappeared. The FBI came to our house, searched through our belongings, read my journal, and confiscated my brother's radio. All Japanese people with one-sixteenth Japanese blood were ordered onto a train bound for a relocation camp "for our protection." We were allowed to carry a suitcase and a bedroll. Our home, furniture, clothing and food, dogs, the old Studebaker I drove to school, the truck my father used on the farm, were left behind. The difference between a relocation camp and a concentration camp? For us, there was no difference.

Related Titles:

Looking Like the Enemy by Mary Matsuda Gruenewald. New Sage Press, 2005

Stubborn Twig: Three Generations in the Life of a Japanese American Family by Lauren Kessler. Random House, 1993; Plume, 1994; Oregon Historical Society, 2005

To Breathe the Sky by Grace Takahashi. Asian American Curriculum Project, 2007

30. Daughter of Madrugada

Author: **Frances M. Wood** grew up in California. Her ancestors include a Mexican grandmother and an Irish grandmother. Wood, a librarian and the author of several novels for young readers, lives in North Carolina.
<www.wincbooks.com/franceswood.htm>

Publication: Delacorte Press, 2002; Thorndike Press, 2004. 162 pages

Genre: Historical Fiction   *Level:* Young Adult

Note: Best Books for the Teen Age (NYPL), Los Angeles Public Library List

Summary: After the United States wins the war with Mexico in 1848, life on her Mexican family's ranch in California is greatly changed for thirteen-year-old Cesa.

Subjects: California—Fiction, California—History, Coming of age, Family life— Fiction,

Read-aloud excerpt: Pages 131 through 133

Booktalk: María Francisca (Cesa) de Haro is thirteen in 1846 when the Mexican-American war ends. Cesa and her family are Californios, hidalgos, lords of the land. They live on El Rancho del Valle de la Madrugada (Ranch of the Valley of Dawn) where they lead a gracious life in which hospitality to strangers is a requirement. If someone needs a horse, they give them a horse. Cesa's great aunt is convent-educated and speaks French as well as Spanish. A resident priest tutors the children. Indian servants tend to the running of the household. Vaqueros take care of the vast numbers of cattle that provide their livelihood. After the end of the war that the Mexicans lost, California and vast amounts of the Southwest that had been Mexico become territories of the United States. The life of the de Haros does not immediately change, but soon gold-seeking Americans begin to appear. The newcomers, a rough lot unused to gracious living or generosity, have no manners. They are contemptuous of the Californios, calling Cesa and her family "dirty Mexicans" and "greasers" and seem not to understand that this land is de Haro land, has been so for generations since the original Spanish land grants. Can the de Haro family survive or will they be destroyed, victims of a far-away war?

Related Titles:

Early Tejano Ranching: Daily Life at Ranchos San José & El Fresnillo by Andrés Sáenz and
Andrés Tijerina. Texas A&M University Press and The University of Texas Institute of
Texan Cultures, 1999

*El Mesquite: A Story of the Early Spanish Settlements Between the Nueces and the Rio
Grande* by Elena Zamora O'Shea. Texas A&M University Press, 2000

Tata: A Voice from the Rio Puerco edited by Nasario García. University of New Mexico
Press, 1994.

31. Donald Duk

Author: **Frank Chin,** Chinese American, is the author of several novels and a short
story collection that won an American Book Award. <www.frankchin.com>

Publication: Coffee House Press, 1991. 173 pages

Genre: Contemporary fiction   *Level:* Adult

Summary: On the eve of Chinese New Year in San Francisco's Chinatown, Donald
Duk attempts to deal with his comical name and his feelings for his cultural heritage.

Subjects: California—Fiction, Chinese American—Fictions, San Francisco,
California

Read-aloud excerpt: Pages 1 through 3

Booktalk: Donald Duk has never liked his name. He hates having the same name as
a cartoon character who doesn't wear pants or shoes. Donald takes tap dance lessons and admires Fred Astaire from the old black-and-white movies. He does not
like Chinatown even though he lives there. He wishes they could skip Chinese New
Year because every year the teachers at his school make a big deal out of this
opportunity to teach about Chinese culture—fireworks and all that. Although they
are supposed to learn about the role of the Chinese in early California history, the
history books call them "passive," "nonassertive," and "vulnerable." Donald dreads
the arrival of Chinese New Year, but this year is going to be different, very different.

Related Titles:

Stanford Wong Flunks Big Time by Lisa Yee. Arthur A. Levine Books, 2005

Tiger's Blood by Laurence Yep. HarperCollins, 2005

32. Double Crossing

Author: **Eve Tal**, Jewish author of several books for young readers, was born in the United States and now lives in a kibbutz in Israel. Tal has worked as a waitress, copy writer, events planner, fundraiser, and secretary. <www.eve-tal.com>

Publication: Cinco Puntos Press, 2005. 261 pages

Genre: Historical Fiction   *Level:* Young Adult

Note: Skipping Stones Honor Award

Summary: In 1905, as life becomes increasingly difficult for Jews in Ukraine, eleven-year-old Raizel and her father flee to America in hopes of earning money to bring the rest of the family there, but her father's health and Orthodox faith become barriers.

Subjects: Emigration and immigration, Fathers and daughters, Jews—Fiction, Ukraine

Read-aloud excerpt: Pages 12 through 14

Booktalk: Raizel Balaban, who is twelve years old in 1905, longs to learn to read. It does not seem fair that her brother Lemmel gets to go to school while she has to stay home and help her mother with housework and taking care of the younger children. Lemmel does not even like going to school! With the pogroms getting worse, her father speeds up his plans to leave the Ukraine and immigrate to the United States to escape being drafted into the Czarist Army. It is decided that Raizel will accompany her father on the long journey. Raizel dares to hope that in America she might have a chance to go to school and learn, but little did she imagine how long and hard their journey would be, how her father's Orthodox Jewish beliefs would bring him close to death, and how their family's future would finally rest on her shoulders.

Related Titles:

Shanghai Shadows by Lois Ruby. Holiday House, 2006

33. Down These Mean Streets

Author: **Piri Thomas**, Puerto Rican, was born Juan Pedro Tomás in New York City. He grew up in Spanish Harlem, was involved in drugs and gangs, served seven years in prison, and became a well-known author and poet. <http://www.cheverote.com/piri.html>

Publication: Knopf, 1967; Vintage Books, 1974, 1991, 1997. 334 pages

Genre: Memoir   *Level:* Adult

Subjects: New York—Biography, Puerto Ricans—Biography, Thomas, Piri, 1928-

Read-aloud excerpt: Pages 47 through 51

Booktalk: I was born Juan Pedro Tomás in New York. They call me Piri. I'm Puerto Rican and because of the tone of my skin and my physical appearance, many have said I look African American. Some members of my family looked white and some looked black and some were in-between. Of course those with the lighter skin had it easier, I thought. I was a part of gangs, dropped out of school, worked on ships, and got hooked on heroin. I was involved in more than one crime, and for the one that turned violent, I got sent to prison. I wrote *Down These Mean Streets* because I wanted to tell how things were for me growing up Puerto Rican in Spanish Harlem during the Depression days. This is my story: the gangs, the fights, the poverty, the prejudice that I encountered, and the lessons I learned.

Related Titles:

Family Installments: Memories of Growing Up Hispanic by Edward Rivera. William Morrow, 1982

Buffalo Nickel by Floyd Salas. Arte Público Press, 1992

34. The Education of Ruby Loonfoot

Author: **Paxton Riddle** is a Cherokee poet, editor, reviewer, copyeditor, and the author of several novels. A member of the Wordcraft Circle of Native Writers and Storytellers, he lives in Connecticut. <www.heartsoundspress.com/contributorspage.htm#paxriddle>

Publication: Five Star, 2002. 349 pages

Genre: Historical Fiction   *Level* Adult

Note: "Best Read of 2002" in *Native American Times*

Summary: In 1957 Ruby Loonfoot, an Ojibwe girl, is sent to a Catholic boarding school for Indians.

Subjects: Boarding schools—Fiction, Catholics—Fiction, Indians of North America—Fiction, Mothers and daughters—Fiction, Ojibwa Indians—Fiction

Read-aloud excerpt: Pages 22 through 25

Booktalk: The year is 1957. Thirteen-year-old Ruby Loonfoot is sent to St. Nicholas, a Catholic boarding school for Indian children. At the school they cut her long hair. Ruby and the other children are always hungry, so hungry that they eat the moldy bread, the oatmeal, and any other poor foods they are provided. The children are routinely humiliated, slapped and beaten, and for "serious" offenses, they may be banished to a dark basement for days. One priest habitually molests the young girls. The frozen bodies of two girls who ran away are found in the snow. When Ruby tries to tell about what is happening, no one believes her except Sister Stephanie. After the summer of that first year, Ruby is forced by her mother to return to St. Nicholas in spite of the objections of her traditional grandmother. Upon her return Ruby discovers that Sister Stephanie no longer teaches there and the basement now contains an electric chair for those who misbehave. Is there no help for Ruby and the others?

Related Titles:

Boarding School Seasons by Brenda J. Child. University of Nebraska Press, 1998

Children of the Dragonfly edited by Robert Bensen. University of Arizona Press, 2001

Stolen from Our Embrace by Suzanne Fournier and Ernie Crey. Douglas & McIntyre, 1997

35. The Eighth Promise: An American Son's Tribute to His Toisanese Mother

Author: **William Poy Lee**, Chinese American, is a lawyer with a doctorate degree. Lee is a full-time writer who lives in Berkeley, California. <www.theeighthpromise.com>

Publication: Rodale, 2007. 315 pages

Genre: Memoir   *Level:* Adult

Subjects: Chinese Americans—Biography, Lee, William Poy, 1950- —Biography, Mothers and sons—Biography

Read-aloud excerpt: Pages viii through x

Booktalk: In 1995 Chinese American William Poy Lee went to Suey Wan Chuen, a village in an area known as Toisan, China to learn about his heritage. Lee's mother was born in this Chinese village where her people had lived for more than a thousand years. She was married and immigrated to San Francisco to join her husband. Before she left her ancestral village, she made eight promises to her mother. She promised to raise her children to be Chinese, to teach them the customs, language, and history of her village. She agreed to find husbands for her sisters, to become an American citizen and bring her mother and brothers to the United States. Her fourth promise was to pass on to her children the dream of a democratic Nationalist China. She agreed to keep her children connected to her village, to keep the Clan Sisterhood traditions alive in her home, and to cook traditional soups to maintain a mind-body balance for her family. The eighth promise was to live her life with compassion for all, her family and all people, and to instill that compassion in her children. This memoir explores how Lee's mother kept her promises.

Related Titles:

Chasing Hepburn by Gus Lee. Harmony Books, 2002

36. Emako Blue

Author: **Brenda Woods**, African American, was born in Ohio and now lives in Los Angeles. She is the author of several award-winning novels. <www.brendawoods.net>

Publication: G. P. Putnam's Sons, 2004. 124 pages

Genre: Contemporary fiction   *Level:* Young Adult

Note: Best Books for Teen (NYPL), IRA Children's Book Award, ALA Quick Picks

Summary: Monterey, Savannah, Jamal, and Eddie never had much to do with each other until Emako Blue shows up at chorus practice, but the lives of the five Los Angeles high school students become intertwined and tragedy tears them apart.

Subjects: African Americans—Fiction, California—Fiction, High schools—Fiction, Interpersonal relations, Schools—Fiction

Read-aloud excerpt: Pages 4 through 9

Booktalk: Monterey, Jamal, Eddie, Savannah, and Emako all make the tryouts for choir at their high school. Monterey and Emako soon become friends. Eddie and Monterey are interested in each other, but Eddie is planning to graduate early and go to an out-of-state college. Emako has a voice so special that she is offered a recording contract a few months later, but her mother insists that she has to graduate from high school first because no one in her family ever has. Emako dreams of buying her mother a house in Malibu and sending her younger brother and sister to private schools where they will be safe from gangs. She wants them to avoid following the path of her older brother and Eddie's older brother who are both involved in gangs. When Jamal decides that Emako is the girl for him despite the fact that he has been dating Gina for a while, Gina's friend Savannah feels compelled to get revenge for her friend by making Emako's life miserable. Then something unthinkably horrible happens.

Related Titles:
Bang! by Sharon G. Flake. Jump at the Sun, 2005
The Skin I'm In by Sharon G. Flake. Jump at the Sun, 1998

37. Emilio

Author: **Julia Mercedes Castilla** is from Bogotá, Colombia. The author of several books of fiction as well as nonfiction articles and stories, Castilla lives in Houston, Texas. <www.juliamercedescastilla.com>

Publication: Piñata Books, 1999. 105 pages

Genre: Contemporary fiction   *Level:* Young Adult

Note: Américas Award commended title

Summary: A young immigrant from Central America finds it difficult to learn English and adjust to life in the big city of Houston, Texas.

Subjects: Central America, Emigration and immigration

Read-aloud excerpt: Pages 1 through 4

Booktalk: Every day Emilio hates school a little bit more. He wishes he could go back to his hometown, his old house, his old life in the country where he was born. His mother and older brother Jaime had come to Houston, Texas, a year ago after his father was killed by guerrillas. Then six months ago Emilio and his little sister Victoria joined the family. Now Emilio hates school because he cannot speak English, bullies pick on him, he has no friends, and he misses his father. His mother now works instead of cooking and looking after the family. It seems like Jaime is getting involved in a gang. When Clara befriends Emilio and asks him to go to a baseball game with her and her friends, he starts to think that maybe he will survive in this country, but at the game he can tell that Clara's friends are feeling sorry for him. His pride causes him to make a mistake. Then he lets down his guard at just the wrong time.

Related Titles:

First Crossing: Stories About Teen Immigrants edited by Donald R. Gallo. Candlewick, 2007

Remix: Conversations with Immigrant Teenagers. Marina Budhos. Henry Holt and Company, 1999

38. Emily Goldberg Learns to Salsa

Author: **Micol Ostow**, who is Puerto Rican and Jewish, lives in New York City where she works as a writer and editor. Ostow is the author of several novels and a book on manners. <www.micolostow.com>

Publication: Razorbill, 2006. 200 pages

Genre: Contemporary fiction   *Level:* Young Adult

Note: Books for the Teen Age (NYPL)

Summary: Forced to stay with her mother in Puerto Rico after her grandmother's funeral, half-Jewish Emily, who has just graduated from high school, does not find it easy to connect with her Puerto Rican heritage and relatives she had never met.

Subjects: Family life—Fiction, Identity, Jews—Fiction, New York—Fiction, Puerto Ricans—Fiction, Racially mixed people—Fiction

Read-aloud excerpt: Pages 9 through 12

Booktalk: Emily Goldberg of Westchester, New York, is familiar with her father's Jewish culture but knows nothing of her mother's Puerto Rican heritage until her Puerto Rican grandmother dies. The family, Emily, her brother Max, her father, and her mother fly to the island for the funeral. It is definitely a different world with Puerto Rican relatives, aunts, uncles, and cousins all over the place. Emily will be glad to get back home to her boyfriend Noah. Besides that, she has to pack for the six-week cross-country road trip that she and her friends Adrienne and Isabel have planned to celebrate their high school graduation. Then the roof falls in. Emily's mother decides to stay with her family for a while to adjust to the passing of her mother. Worst of all, Emily has to stay too. Stuck in a "foreign country" in her Spanish-speaking aunt's crowded house with eighteen-year-old cousin Lucy who clearly does not like her, Emily's summer seems likely to be a disaster.

Related Titles:
Border Crossing by Maria Colleen Cruz. Piñata Books, 2003

39. Estrella's Quinceañera

Author: **Malín Alegría** is a Mexican American who grew up in the San Francisco area. Alegría is a dancer, performer, teacher, and writer. She lives in New Mexico and California. <www.malinalegria.com/Casa.html>

Publication: Simon & Schuster Books for Young Readers, 2006. 260 pages

Genre: Contemporary fiction   **Level:** Young Adult

Summary: Estrella's mother and aunt are planning a gaudy, traditional quinceañera for her, even though it is the last thing she wants.

Subjects: Friendship, Mexican Americans—Fiction, Mothers and daughters—Fiction, Quinceañera (Social custom)

Read-aloud excerpt: Pages 1 through 4

Booktalk: Things are not going well for Estrella Alvarez as her fifteenth birthday approaches. She does not want a quinceañera, but it means a lot to her mother. Her mother did not have a quinceañera because her family could not afford one. Now her mom wants Estrella to have a traditional fifteenth birthday celebration although their family cannot afford it. Then there is the problem with her friends. Estrella's classmates at her upscale new school are rich, not like her old friends from the barrio. Make that the old friends she used to have. Tere and Izzy are mad at her because she has been hanging out with Christie and Sheila, two rich white girls who are students at Sacred Heart. Estrella can just imagine what they would think if they saw her house and met her family. Then Speedy, a guy she remembers from grade school, turns up in her life. He is interesting, but her parents will not allow her to date until she is sixteen. Sheila and Christie know a boy they think she should meet. Can her life get any more complicated?

Related Titles:

Fifteen Candles edited by Adriana Lopez. Harper, 2007

Once Upon a Quinceañera: Coming of Age in the USA by Julia Alvarez. Viking, 2007

40. Finding Miracles

Author: **Julia Alvarez,** of Dominican descent, was born in New York and spent some of her childhood in the Dominican Republic. The author of novels, essays, poetry, and picture books, Alvarez lives on a farm in Vermont. <www.juliaalvarez.com>

Publication: Knopf, 2004. 264 pages

Genre: Contemporary fiction   *Level:* Young Adult

Note: Texas TAYSHAS List, Oklahoma Sequoyah List

Summary: Fifteen-year-old Milly Kaufman is an average American teenager until Pablo, a new student at her school, inspires her to search for her birth family in his native country.

Subjects: Adoption, Central America, High Schools—Fiction, Schools—Fiction

Read-aloud excerpt: Pages 3 through 6

Booktalk: My name is Milly Kaufman. Well, actually the name pinned to the blanket that I was wrapped in when the nuns found me on the doorstep of the orphanage was Milagros, which is the Spanish word for miracles. I was born in another country and adopted by the Kaufmans as a baby after my adopted mother saw me at that orphanage. The only clues we have about my past are in a mahogany box that my parents keep in their bedroom. I could look in that box any time, but I have not felt that it is the right time yet. Not many people in this little Vermont town know that I am adopted. When I think about that, my hands start itching and breaking out in an ugly red rash, so I usually try not to think about those things. Then a boy named Pablo Bolívar checked into our class at school. As soon as I saw him and he saw me, I knew there was trouble ahead.

Related Titles:

A Single Square Picture: A Korean Adoptee's Search for Her Roots by Katy Robinson. Berkley Books, 2002

41. Finding My Hat

Author: **John Son** was born in Germany to Korean parents. He immigrated to the United States as a child and has lived in Houston, Memphis, Chicago, and New York City. <www.kidsreads.com/series/series-first-person-author.asp#Son>

Publication: Orchard Books 2003. 184 pages

Genre: Contemporary fiction   *Level:* Young Adult

Note: First Person Fiction series. Best Books for the Teen Age (NYPL)

Summary: Jin-Han describes growing up with his mother and father, immigrants from Korea, and his little sister as they move to different cities with his parents' business.

Subjects: Family life—Fiction, Korean Americans—Fiction

Read-aloud excerpt: Pages 130 through 133

Booktalk: Jin-Han's parents immigrated to the United States from Korea by way of Germany. Although both were educated people, they found themselves owners of a wig shop which they operated to make a living for the family. During the first years of Jin-Han's life, they lived in Chicago, then Memphis (home of Elvis Presley), and finally Houston. Jin-Han went to nursery school, then elementary, and junior high. As he matured, Jin-Han struggled to understand the people around him, his parents, those who considered him and his family "different," and friendships with boys and girls. Just as he began to find his place in life, something horrible happened that would forever alter life as he had known it.

Related Titles:
F Is for Fabuloso by Marie G. Lee. HarperCollins, 1999

42. Finding My Voice

Author: **Marie G. Lee** was born in Minnesota. She is Korean American. Lee is the author of several novels for young adults and a founder of the Asian American Writers Workshop.
<www.harpercollins.com/authors/17389/Marie_G_Lee/index.aspx>

Publication: Houghton Mifflin, 1992. 165 pages

Genre: Contemporary fiction   *Level:* Young Adult

Note: Best Books for Reluctant Readers (ALA)

Summary: As she tries to enjoy her senior year and choose a college, Korean American Ellen Sung must deal with classmates' prejudice and pressure from her parents.

Subjects: High schools—Fiction, Korean Americans—Fiction, Prejudices, Schools—Fiction

Read-aloud excerpt: Pages 144 through 145

Booktalk: Ellen Sung, Korean American, lives in a small town in Minnesota where there are few Asian people. Her parents are immigrants who want her to follow in her older sister's footsteps and go to Harvard. This is her senior year, and Ellen is not sure what she wants. She would like to continue gymnastics, but her father will not allow that if she does not get A's in all her classes. When classmates on the bus and in the halls harass her and call her chink, and teachers make jokes about Koreans eating dogs, Ellen never knows how to respond. She does not like to make a fuss. She just wishes things like that would not happen, but they do happen, time and again. It would be great to get away from this small town with few opportunities and its prejudiced people, but does she want to go to Harvard? Can she get into Harvard if she decides that is what she wants? If she decides to choose another path, can she find the strength to defy her parents? Can she find her own voice?

Related Titles:

Saying Goodbye by Marie G. Lee. Houghton Mifflin, 1994

Somebody's Daughter by Marie Myung-Ok Lee. Beacon Press, 2005

43. Flight

Author: **Sherman Alexie,** author of numerous novels and short story collections, is of Spokane and Coeur d'Alene descent. Alexie, who wrote the screenplay for a film, *Smoke Signals*, based on his short stories, lives in Seattle. <www.shermanalexie.com>

Publication: Black Cat/Grove, 2007. 181 pages

Genre: Contemporary fiction   *Level:* Adult

Summary: A half-Indian, half-Irish boy nicknamed Zits goes from foster home to foster home and travels through time and space.

Subjects: Foster children—Fiction, Indians of North America—Fiction

Read-aloud excerpt: Pages 7 through 9.

Booktalk: They call me Zits. My father was an Indian and a drunk. My Irish mother died of breast cancer. I've lived in twenty foster homes and been in more schools than that. Everything I own, pants, shirts, underwear, hat, socks, photographs, and three paperback books, fits into a single backpack. The books? *The Dead Zone, Winter in the Blood,* and *Grapes of Wrath.* I get in lots of fights and arguments, and I like to start fires. I shoplift a lot, anything that I can stuff into my pockets. I always get caught, and they put me in juvenile jail. This morning I woke up in another strange bedroom, my twenty-first foster home. I go into the bathroom, stare at myself in the mirror, and count the zits on my face. This house has no books. What kind of life will I have in a house with no books? At breakfast I exchange words with my new foster father and push my new foster mother against the wall. Then I run and run until the police chase me down and handcuff me. At the jail they put me in a holding cell with three other kids. One black, one white, and one Chinese, a regular United Nations right here in Seattle's Central District. That is where I meet Justice, get my hands on a couple of guns, and start to travel.

Related Titles:
The Lone Ranger and Tonto Fistfight in Heaven by Sherman Alexie. Grove Press, 2005

44. Flight to Freedom

Author: **Ana Veciana-Suarez**, Cuban American, emigrated to the U.S. with her parents when she was six. A syndicated columnist in Florida, she has worked as a writer, reporter, and editor. <www.anaveciana-suarez.com>

Publication: Orchard Books, 2002. 215 pages

Genre: Contemporary fiction   *Level:* Young Adult

Note: First Person Fiction series, Américas Award commended

Summary: Writing in the diary her father gave her, thirteen-year-old Yara describes life with her family in Havana, Cuba, in 1967 and her experiences in Florida, after immigrating there to be with some relatives while leaving others behind.

Subjects: Cuban Americans—Fiction, Diaries, Emigration and immigration, Florida—Fiction, Immigrants—Fiction

Read-aloud excerpt: Pages 138 through 140

Booktalk: Yara García is thirteen years old in 1967 when she starts writing in her diary. She and her older sister Ileana and her younger sister Ana María live with their parents in Havana, Cuba. Because her father has requested permission for them to leave the country, Yara and her family are called *gusanos* or *worms* for their desire to leave Cuba and go into exile in Miami, Florida. Yara's father is not a communist and does not agree with Fidel Castro's form of government. After several months of waiting, they receive their exit visas and fly to Miami. Soon the family finds a place to live with relatives, the children are given donated clothes, and the girls start to school. Yara's dad insists that they are in the United States only temporarily and that they will be returning to Cuba soon. Her mother finds a job, starts to take classes to learn English, and secretly is learning to drive a car. The girls gradually begin to fit in with their classmates, but Mr. García seems determined to cling to the past causing much discord in the family.

Related Titles:
Birthday Parties in Heaven: Thoughts on Love, Life, Grief, and Other Matters of the Heart
   by Ana Veciana-Suarez. Plume, 2000

45. The Flood

Author: **Carol Ascher**, daughter of Jewish refugee parents, is a research scientist at New York University. Her field of research is schools and education. Ascher, author of fiction and nonfiction, lives in New York.
<www.curbstone.org/authdetail.cfm?AuthID=9>

Publication: Crossing Press, 1987; Curbstone Press, 1996. 183 pages

Genre: Historical fiction   *Level:* Adult

Summary: In 1951 Eva Hoffman, daughter of Austrian Jewish refugees, is in Topeka, Kansas, when Brown v. Topeka Board of Education, a school desegregation case, is tried in a local court.

Subjects: Antisemitism—Fiction, Children of Holocaust survivors—Fiction, Jews—Fiction, Kansas

Read-aloud excerpt: Pages 1 through 3

Booktalk: Eva Hoffman, daughter of Jewish refugees, lives in Kansas in 1951. Eva's family is Jewish but they do not attend a synagogue or carry out Jewish traditions. They are secular, her father says. Some things about her family's past are never discussed. Eva has visited some of the Christian churches that most people in their town go to. When her mother forgets and speaks German, Eva is embarrassed. Sometimes when her mother tells people about how she and her husband left Europe with almost nothing, Eva interrupts and changes the subject. When Mrs. Johnson, the Negro woman who cleans their house, tells about her daughter who is going to lose her job as a teacher at the colored school if the court case that Reverend Brown is bringing against the Board of Education abolishes segregation, Eva realizes there are no Negroes in her school or at any of the churches she has visited. Rains continue day after day, week after week, until finally the river floods. Homes are damaged or destroyed, and lives are disrupted. Eva's parents generously invite a displaced white family to share their home temporarily. Now the prejudice that has surrounded them is inside their own home, living with them.

Related Titles:
Speed of Light by Sybil Rosen. Atheneum, 1999

46. Fresh Off the Boat

Author: **Melissa de la Cruz** was born in Manila and grew up in California. De la Cruz has worked as a computer programmer and financial consultant and is a full-time writer, the author of several novels and nonfiction. <www.melissa-delacruz.com>

Publication: HarperCollins, 2005. 243 pages

Genre: Contemporary fiction   *Level:* Young Adult

Summary: When her family emigrates from the Philippines to San Francisco, fourteen-year-old Vicenza Arambullo struggles to fit in at her exclusive, all-girl private school.

Subjects: California—Fiction, Filipino Americans—Fiction, High schools—Fiction, Immigrants—Fiction, Moving, Household, San Francisco, California, Schools—Fiction

Read-aloud excerpt: Pages 85 through 87

Booktalk: Vicenza Arambullo's life has changed drastically since her family left Manila and came to the U.S. Back there her father was a respected man, her mother dressed well, and the family had money. Now her dad's import business is taking in almost no money, her mother operates a small cafeteria at a mall, and the women of the family shop at the Salvation Army thrift store. The family drives a beat-up old Dodge van, but Vicenza attends Grosvenor, a very expensive school, where snobby popular girls like Whitney, Georgia, and Trish make fun of Vicenza or totally ignore her. She has a huge crush on Claude Caligari, who doesn't seem to know she is alive even though she sits next to him in geometry class. As Vicenza sends lie after lie via e-mail to her friend Peaches back in Manila, she wonders if she will ever be anything other than FOB, fresh off the boat.

Related Titles:
Danger and Beauty by Jessica Hagedorn. City Lights Books, 2002
Going Home to a Landscape: Writings by Filipinas edited by Marianne Villanueva and
     Virginia Cerenio. CALYX Books, 2003

47. Getting It

Author: **Alex Sanchez** was born in Mexico to parents of Cuban and German descent. He has a master's degree in guidance and counseling and is the author of six novels for young adults. His book *So Hard to Say* won a Lambda Award. <www.alexsanchez.com>

Publication: Simon & Schuster Books for Young Readers, 2006. 211 pages

Genre: Contemporary fiction   *Level:* Young Adult

Note: Books for the Teen Age (NYPL), International Latino Book Award

Summary: Hoping to impress a sexy female classmate, fifteen-year-old Carlos secretly hires gay student Sal to give him an image makeover, in exchange for Carlos's help in forming a Gay-Straight Alliance at their Texas high school.

Subjects: Coming of age, Friendship, High Schools—Fiction, Homosexuality, Mexican Americans—Fiction, Schools—Fiction

Read-aloud excerpt: Pages 15 through 16

Booktalk: Carlos is fifteen. He wants a girlfriend and all that goes along with that. Roxana is his dream girl although she doesn't know it. She is hot and Carlos, well, Carlos, is not hot. His friends Pulga, Playboy, and Toro all have, or have had, girls but Carlos never. He wants to change that, but how? He has no one to go to for advice. His dad and mom are divorced. His dad has a new wife and a baby boy and does not have time for Carlos even when they spend the weekends together. Carlos's mother has a boyfriend, and besides, she is a woman so it would be too embarrassing to explain things to her. Of course he cannot talk to his friends, but he really needs help to get Roxana to notice him. After he sees Sal so at ease with girls, Carlos starts to think. Sal may be gay or not. Just because everybody says he is does not really prove anything. Sal dresses well and seems very sure of himself. Carlos does not dress well, cannot talk to girls, and is definitely not sure of himself. Maybe Sal would help him like on that television show where gay guys help give straight guys makeovers. Yeah, it is a crazy idea, but maybe.

Related Titles:

The God Box by Alex Sanchez, Simon & Schuster, 2007
Rainbow Boys by Alex Sanchez. Simon & Schuster, 2001
Tommy Stands Alone by Gloria Velásquez. Piñata Books, 1995

48. Girls for Breakfast

Author: **David Yoo**, Korean American, lives in Massachusetts. *Girls for Breakfast* is his first novel. <www.daveyoo.com/html/index.html>

Publication: Delacorte Press, 2005. 294 pages

Genre: Contemporary fiction   *Level:* Young Adult

Note: Books for the Teen Age (NYPL)

Summary: As he reflects on his life in Renfield, Connecticut, on his high school graduation day, Nick Park wonders how much being the only Asian American in school affected his thwarted quest for popularity and a girlfriend.

Subjects: High schools—Fiction, Identity, Korean Americans—Fiction, Popularity, Prejudices, Schools—Fiction

Read-aloud excerpt: Pages 102 through 106

Booktalk: This could conceivably be the most important day of Nick Park's life. Today is his graduation day. Standing on top of the water tower behind his house in Renfield, Connecticut, Nick is skipping commencement rehearsal. He is missing from the group, as usual, the only Asian American in the graduating class. What will people say when he does not show up for graduation? When did things start to go so wrong in his life? Was it in third grade when he accidentally killed Marvin, the class hamster? When he lied about being a kung fu master? At the fifth grade Immigrant Fair when he ditched the kimchee and rice his mother had made and took two boxes of macaroni and cheese to represent his culture? When he stole his friend's dad's *Playboy* magazines and his friend got blamed? When Grace at the Korean church called him a banana, yellow on the outside, white on the inside? When he was embarrassed to be seen with the less-popular guys and less-than-perfect girls? Why the lifelong need to be accepted as just Nick, not the Asian?

Related Titles:
Necessary Roughness by Marie G. Lee. HarperCollins, 1996

49. Habibi

Author: **Naomi Shihab Nye**, Palestinian American, is a poet and the author and editor of several books. Of Arab and American descent, Nye lives in San Antonio, Texas. <www.barclayagency.com/nye.html>

Publication: Simon & Schuster Books for Young Readers, 1997. 259 pages

Genre: Contemporary fiction   *Level:* Young Adult

Note: Best Books for Young Adults (ALA), Jane Addams Book Award

Summary: When Liyana Abboud, her younger brother, and her parents move from St. Louis to a home between Jerusalem and the Palestinian village where her father was born, they must deal with the tensions between Jews and Palestinians.

Subjects: Emigration and immigration, Family life—Fiction, Jerusalem, Jewish-Arab relations

Read-aloud excerpt: Pages 1 through 3.

Booktalk: Liyana Abboud is fourteen the night of the special family meeting at a diner near their home in St. Louis. The school year is nearing its end. Next year Liyana will be going to high school and her brother Rafik will be going to middle school. Their family has reached a crossroads, their parents say. They have decided to move to Jerusalem where their father will work. There they will be near Liyana's Arab grandmother and the rest of her father's family who still live in Palestine, which is now known as Israel. This will be a good time for the family to move back to her father's homeland, their parents believe. This is not, Liyana thinks to herself, a good time for her to leave the only home she has ever known. Just last night she had been kissed by a boy for the first time and she was looking forward to another kiss. Her father had been an immigrant to the United States years before, before he met their mother Susan, before Liyana and Rafik. Now Liyana and her brother, Arab Americans, will become immigrants. They will be going to a country in which Arabs are a minority, a country in which they may not be welcome.

Related Titles:

Running on Eggs by Anna Levine. Front Street, 1999

50. Hunger of Memory: The Education of Richard Rodriguez: An Autobiography

Author: **Richard Rodriguez**, Mexican American, grew up in California. He is a writer for newspapers and magazines, an editor and columnist, and the author of three books. <www.pbs.org/newshour/indepth_coverage/entertainment/essays/essayist_rodriguez.html>

Publication: D.R. Godine, 1982; Bantam Books, 2004. 195 pages

Genre: Memoir   *Level:* Adult

Note: Christopher Prize for Autobiography, Anisfeld-Wolf Prize for Civil Rights

Subjects: California—Biography, Mexican Americans—Biography, Rodriguez, Richard

Read-aloud excerpt: Pages 61 through 63

Booktalk: My name is Richard Rodriguez. This is the first of three memoirs or autobiographies that I have written. Included in *Hunger of Memory* are thoughts and memories of my early years. I was born in California, the third child of Mexican immigrant parents. The language we spoke in our home was Spanish. When I started to school, I moved into an English-speaking world. After a few months in which I did not speak at all at school, the nuns visited my parents and asked them to speak English to us at home. From that time on, things changed in our house. We spoke English, my parents, my brothers and sisters, and I. Without a doubt that helped me become a better student but it changed the way we children saw and treated our parents. Things were never the same between us after that, but I think it had to happen that way. In this intellectual autobiography, I also write my thoughts about bilingual education, college and being a minority student, books and reading, being a scholarship boy, religion, outward appearance, light or dark skin, and family secrets.

Related Titles:

Brown: The Last Discovery of America by Richard Rodriguez. Viking, 2002
Days of Obligation: An Argument with My Mexican Father by Richard Rodriguez. Viking, 1992.
On Borrowed Words: A Memoir of Language by Ilan Stavans. Viking, 2001

51. If You Come Softly

Author: **Jacqueline Woodson**, African American, was born in Ohio but grew up in South Carolina and Brooklyn. Woodson is the author of many award-winning books for children and young adults. <www.jacquelinewoodson.com/contact.shtml>

Publication: G. P. Putnam's Sons, 1998. 181 pages

Genre: Contemporary fiction   *Level:* Young Adult

Note: Best Books for Young Adults (ALA)

Summary: After meeting at a private school, fifteen-year-old Jeremiah, and Ellie who is white, fall in love.

Subjects: African Americans—Fiction, Family life—Fiction, Interracial dating, New York—Fiction, Schools—Fiction

Read-aloud excerpt: Pages 51 through 58

Booktalk: Ellie Eisen is white. Jeremiah Roselind is black. Ellie is the youngest of her family, the baby, the only child still living at home. Her dad is a hard-working doctor. Her mother is an unhappy woman who has left her family twice. There is always the possibility that she might leave again. Jeremiah is an only child. His father is a famous film maker. His mother has written three books. His mother and father live in separate apartments, and his father lives with another woman. Jeremiah is required by law to spend equal time with each of his parents. When Ellie and Miah both start the new school year at Percy, an exclusive private school, their paths cross by accident but each remembers the moment that they met and fell in love. As their friendship grows, it seems the whole entire world, classmates, friends, strangers on the street, disapproves, but with each meeting, Ellie and Miah are more sure that they do love each other. Can they overcome the odds? Will their love survive? Will it be forever?

Related Titles:
The Dear One by Jacqueline Woodson. G. P. Putnam's Sons, 2004

52. In the Break

Author: **Jack Lopez** is a Mexican American who grew up in California where he surfed on the beaches. A writer whose works have appeared in anthologies, collections, and literary magazines, he teaches creative writing at a university. <www.jacklopez.net>

Publication: Little, Brown, 2006. 192 pages

Genre: Contemporary fiction   *Level:* Young Adult

Summary: Surfing is Juan Barrela's life but when his friend Jamie faces a violent home situation, Juan steals his mother's car and drives to Mexico to help him hide.

Subjects: Best friends, California—Fiction, Friendship, Mexican Americans—Fiction, Surfing

Read-aloud excerpt: Pages 20 through 22

Booktalk: I am Juan Barrela. I am fifteen. My friend Jamie and I are surfers. Jamie's sister Amber has gotten into surfing, too. Their dad died a few years ago in a freeway accident. That was a bad time, but things got better at their house after their mother married "F." Their step dad's name is Frederick, but we call him something else. Anyway, we just call him "F" for short. "F" was okay for awhile and then he started turning into this scary fury-filled drill instructor kind of a guy. That early September morning Jamie's mom's car would not run so he borrowed "F"'s car, without asking, to get us all to the beach for some early morning surfing. Then "F" showed up yelling and cursing and when he was about to grab Amber, Jamie shoved him and punches were exchanged before Jamie and "F" took off up the Coast Highway. That night Amber showed up at my house and told me what had gone down. I knew I had to help Jamie even if it meant borrowing my mom's car in the middle of the night. I will have it back early tomorrow, I thought. Dad is at work and everybody else is asleep so I will do what I have to do and be back home before anybody knows the car is gone. That is what I thought.

Related Titles:
Buried Onions by Gary Soto. Harcourt, 1997

53. Indian Boyhood

Author: **Charles A. Eastman**, born in 1858 in Minnesota, was given the Dakota Sioux name Ohiyesa, Winner. Raised by his grandmother, he became a doctor and treated the injured at Wounded Knee in 1890.
<www.kstrom.net/isk/stories/authors/eastman.html>

Publication: McClure, Philips & Co., 1902; Little Brown, 1939; Dover Publications, 1971; Rio Grande Press, 1976; University of Nebraska Press, 1991; Time-Life Books, 1993. 247 pages

Genre: Memoir   *Level:* Adult

Note: First Indian Achievement Award, 1933

Summary: A Santee Sioux Indian describes his childhood experiences and training as a warrior in the late nineteenth century until he was taken to live in the white man's world.

Subjects: Eastman, Charles Alexander, 1858-1939, Indians of North America—Biography, Santee Indians—Biography

Read-aloud excerpt: Pages 3 through 5

Booktalk: I was born in 1858 in southwestern Minnesota. My first name was Hakadah, Pitiful Last One, because my mother died soon after I was born. My mother gave me to my father's mother when she knew she was leaving this world. She knew that her mother would not be able to raise me but my other grandmother would. My people were Sioux. I lived among my people until I was fifteen. This book records some of what I learned about traditional Indian life as a boy before I became acquainted with "civilization."

Related Titles:
Goodbird the Indian: His Story by Edward Goodbird and Gilbert L. Wilson. Minnesota
    Historical Society Press, 1985
Indian Heroes and Great Chieftains by Charles A. Eastman (Ohiyesa). Dover, 1997

54. Jimi & Me

Author: **Jaime Adoff** is of mixed descent. His mother, Virginia Hamilton, was African American. His dad, Arnold Adoff, is Anglo American. Jaime, a musician, writer, poet, and songwriter, lives in Ohio. <www.jaimeadoff.com/bio.htm>

Publication: Jump at the Sun/Hyperion, 2005, 2007. 336 pages

Genre: Contemporary fiction   *Level:* Young Adult

Note: Coretta Scott King Award, John Steptoe New Talent Author

Summary: After his father's death, Keith James moves from Brooklyn to a Midwestern town where his mixed race heritage is not accepted.

Subjects: African Americans—Fiction, Fathers and sons, Grief, Hendrix, Jimi, Racially mixed people—Fiction

Read-aloud excerpt: Pages 50 through 54

Booktalk: Keith James is thirteen years old when his music-producer dad is killed in a robbery just because he happened to be first in line to pay for his diet cola. Grief-stricken and shocked, Keith and his mother soon learn that there is no money. Within a month, they have to leave their home in Brooklyn, winding up in Hollow Falls, Ohio, in a small apartment with Aunt Berny. Keith's love of Jimi Hendrix, his caramel brown skin, tie-dyed psychedelic shirts, bell-bottom pants, and afro hair do not help him fit in at Hollow Falls Junior High. When beautiful blonde Veronica befriends Keith, things get worse. The local kids do not approve because Keith is biracial and Veronica is white. Things are grim. Then when Keith and his mother learn that his father had a secret life, it seems like Keith is losing his dad all over again.

Related Titles:

Black White and Jewish by Rebecca Walker. Riverhead Books, 2001

The Sweeter the Juice: A Family Memoir in Black and White by Shirlee Taylor Haizlip. Simon & Schuster, 1994

55. The Jumping Tree

Author: **René Saldaña, Jr.,** Mexican American, grew up in Texas. Saldaña has taught in schools and colleges in Texas and Georgia and is the author of several books. He teaches at a university in Texas where he lives with his family. <http://rsaldanajr.com>

Publication: Delacorte Press, 2001. 181 pages

Genre: Contemporary fiction   *Level:* Young Adult

Note: Américas Award commended

Summary: Rey, a Mexican American living with his close-knit family in a Texas town near the Mexican border, describes his transition from boy to young man.

Subjects: Family life—Fiction, Fathers and sons, Mexican Americans—Fiction, Texas—Fiction

Read-aloud excerpt: Pages 126 through 129

Booktalk: Rey Castañeda grows up in Nuevo Peñitas, a small town in deep south Texas near the Mexican border. As a child he is surrounded by family, extended family, and friends. When he starts junior high school, Rey has to endure many embarrassments. He has to wear a pair of hideous red-orange boots that his father picked out for him. A girl pledges eternal love but loses interest before Rey can give her a very special

Valentine gift. His longtime friend Chuy gets mixed up with drugs, is arrested for stealing, and then expelled from school. By the time he is in eighth grade, Rey has begun to see the hard realities of life beyond his small world of family and friends. From those early experiences, he comes to understand the prejudices of the outside world and to appreciate what it takes to become a real man.

Related Titles:
Crazy Loco: Stories by David Rice. Dial Books, 2001

56. Lorenzo's Secret Mission

Authors: **Lila and Rick Guzmán** Rick Guzmán is a Mexican American Texan, a lawyer, and a writer. Lila Guzmán, writer, wife of Rick, is the author of fiction and a series of nonfiction biographies of famous Latinos. They live in Texas. <www.lilaguzman.com>

Publication: Piñata Books, 2001. 153 pages

Genre: Historical Fiction   *Level:* Young Adult

Note: Historical figures Bernardo de Gálvez and George Gibson are characters in the book.

Summary: In 1776, fifteen-year-old Lorenzo Bannister leaves Texas and his father's new grave to carry a letter to the Virginia grandfather he has never known, and becomes involved with the struggle of the American Continental Army and its Spanish supporters.

Subjects: Gálvez, Bernardo de, 1746-1786, Gibson, George, 1747-1791, Identity, Orphans—Fiction, Slavery—Fiction, United States—History

Read-aloud excerpt: Pages 22 through 24

Booktalk: Lorenzo Bannister was fifteen years old in August, 1776, when his father died. To honor his father's deathbed wish, Lorenzo leaves the Spanish mission in San Antonio and sets out for Virginia to deliver a letter to the grandfather he has never known. Attacked in New Orleans by pirates, he escapes. As he is seeking a ship bound for Virginia, he meets a beautiful young French girl named Eugenie, gets into a fight with British marines, and is arrested and thrown into jail by Spanish soldiers. As events unfold, Lorenzo meets Bernardo de Gálvez and George Gibson and becomes involved in a series of adventures as he joins with others in an attempt to deliver medicine and gunpowder to George Washington's army.

Related Titles:
Lorenzo's Revolutionary Quest by Lila and Rick Guzmán. Piñata Books, 2003
Lorenzo and the Turncoat by Lila and Rick Guzmán. Piñata Books, 2006

57. Loves Me, Loves Me Not

Author: **Anilú Bernardo**, a Cuban American originally from Santiago, Cuba, is the author of several books for young adults and adults. She lives in Florida with her family. <http://www.childrenslit.com/childrenslit/f_anilubernardo.html>

Publication: Piñata Books/Arte Público Press, 1998. 169 pages

Genre: Contemporary fiction   *Level:* Young Adult

Note: Books for the Teen Age (NYPL), YALSA Popular Paperbacks

Summary: While trying to win the attention of a high school basketball star, Maggie, a Cuban American, learns painful lessons about romantic young love.

Subjects: Best friends, Cuban Americans—Fiction, High schools—Fiction, Interpersonal relations, Schools—Fiction

Read-aloud excerpt: Pages 15 through 19

Booktalk: Cuban American Maggie Castillo is secretly in love with tall, blond basketball player Zack. She and Zack are in the same German class. He actually sits beside her sometimes, and he once asked to borrow her German notebook. Maggie, who wants to become a nurse like her mother, is sure that he will eventually see how special she is. When she begins part-time work after school as a nursing assistant to elderly Mrs. Maxwell, who turns out to be Zack's grandmother, Maggie is convinced that destiny has brought them together! Although Zack sometimes makes teasing remarks about Cubans, Maggie does not believe he is really prejudiced as some of her friends say he is. Then she meets Justin, a new guy at their school. Justin is definitely interested in her and soon asks her out on a double date with her friend Susie and his friend Carlos. After that date, Maggie is confused. Justin is nice but what about her true love, Zack?

Related Titles:

The Chin Kiss King by Ana Veciana-Suarez. Farrar, Straus & Giroux, 1997

58. Madame Ambassador: The Shoemaker's Daughter

Author: **Mari-Luci Jaramillo**, Mexican American, worked as a teacher, vice president of a university, ambassador, and deputy assistant secretary of state, before retiring.
<http://www.asu.edu/brp/recent/MLJar.html>

Publication: Bilingual Review/Press, 2002. 178 pages

Genre: Memoir   *Level:* Adult

Subjects: Ambassadors—United States, Honduras, Jaramillo, Mari-Luci, Mexican Americans—Biography, Women ambassadors, Women civil rights workers

Read-aloud excerpt: Pages 1 through 4

Booktalk: Mari-Luci Jaramillo was born in Las Vegas, New Mexico. Her mother was of Spanish descent and her father was Mexican. During her childhood, Las Vegas was divided by invisible lines that separated the Anglo, Jewish, Syrian, and Spanish-speaking communities. Mari-Luci's family was poor. She started to school wearing clothing her mother had made from flour sacks. The soles of her shoes were cardboard. Children in the school attended segregated classes. At lunch Mari-Luci and her friends hid their flour tortillas in brown paper bags because they knew they would be ridiculed if the other children saw their food. From this humble background Mari-Luci went on to graduate from high school and then college. This memoir is her account of how a shoemaker's daughter from New Mexico earned a Ph.D. degree, became a teacher and a university administrator, and then the first Mexican American ambassador to a Latin American country.

Related Titles:

All Pianos Have Keys and Other Stories by José A. Cárdenas. Intercultural Development Research Association, 1994

Julian Nava: My Mexican-American Journey by Julian Nava. Arte Público Press, 2002

My Spanish-Speaking Left Foot by José A. Cárdenas. Intercultural Development Research Association, 1997

59. The Making of a Civil Rights Leader

Author: **José Angel Gutiérrez** grew up as a Mexican American in Texas where he began his lifelong work in civil rights. A lawyer, author, editor, and teacher, he lives in Texas.
<www.americanpatrol.com/REFERENCE/JoseAngelGutierrezQuote.html>

Publication: Piñata Books, 2005. 125 pages

Genre: Memoir   *Level:* Young Adult

Note: Author named an "Outstanding Latino Texan of the 20th Century"

Subjects: Civil rights workers, Crystal City, Texas, Gutiérrez, José Angel, Mexican Americans—Biography, Political activists—Biography, Texas—Biography

Read-aloud excerpt: Pages vii through viii

Booktalk: Who am I? My name is José Angel Gutiérrez. I was born in Crystal City, Texas. My father was a doctor who traveled with Pancho Villa's army in Mexico in the early 1900s. My mother was a native Texan. Growing up in Crystal City, I struggled with who I was supposed to be. I was Mexican American but being Mexican was not a good thing in that time and that place. When I started to school, I and my friends were punished if we spoke Spanish in the school buildings or on the playground. The Anglos in charge of the schools wanted to push us out. They wanted us to become dropouts. I did not drop out, but I did become an Anglo because that was the only way I could survive and succeed in that school system. In spite of continual opposition, in spite of being placed in vocational classes, and in spite of the preferential treatment the Anglos received in elementary and high school, I did graduate. I earned a college degree and then another and another. Eventually I earned a doctorate degree, became a lawyer and a university professor, started a political party, and became president of the Crystal City school board. This is the story of how I combined the three parts of myself, Mexican, Anglo, and Chicano, and became a civil rights leader.

Related Titles:

Crossing Guadalupe Street: Growing Up Hispanic & Protestant by David Maldonado, Jr. University of New Mexico Press, 2001

A Darker Shade of Crimson: Odyssey of a Harvard Chicano by Ruben Navarrette, Jr. Bantam, 1993

Memories of Chicano History: The Life and Narrative of Bert Corona by Mario T. García. University of California Press, 1994

We Won't Back Down! Severita Lara's Rise from Student Leader to Mayor by José Angel Gutiérrez. Arte Público Press, 2005

60. Mama's Girl

Author: **Veronica Chambers** refers to herself as "Latinegra" because of her African American and Latina heritage. Her parents were Panamanian and Dominican. Chambers is a magazine editor and a writer. <http://veronicachambers.com>

Publication: Riverhead Books, 1996. 194 pages

Genre: Memoir   *Level:* Adult

Note: Best Books for Young Adults (ALA)

Subjects: Chambers, Veronica, New York—Biography, Panamanian Americans—Biography

Read-aloud excerpt: Pages 51 through 53

Booktalk: Veronica's mother grew up in Panama. Her father was born in the Dominican Republic but moved to the U.S. when he was twelve. He met his wife while he was an Army soldier stationed in Panama. When Veronica was five, her father left the military and the family moved to Brooklyn where they lived for several years. Her parents' marriage was troubled. Her father frequently beat her mother and neglected his children. After their divorce, Veronica's mother had to struggle to provide for her children. Because of her lack of education, she worked hard at low-paying jobs. Veronica frequently felt that neither of her parents cared for her, but she was a good student in spite of the difficulties at home and the lack of support for her dreams and ambitions. This memoir is her account of growing up in a troubled home, moving from school to school, and overcoming abuse and neglect to become a successful, educated professional woman.

Related Titles:

Caucasia by Danzy Senna. Riverhead Books, 1998

Project Girl by Janet McDonald. Farrar, Straus and Giroux, 1999

61. Mayhem Was Our Business/Memorias de un veterano

Author: Sabine R. Ulibarrí, Mexican American, was born in New Mexico, in 1919. The author of fiction, essays, and poetry in English and in Spanish, and a university professor, Ulibarrí died in 2003.

<http://elibrary.unm.edu/oanm/NmU/nmu1%23mss561bc/nmu1%23mss561bc_m4.html>

Publication: Bilingual Press, 1997. 115 pages

Genre: Memoir   **Level:** Adult

Note: Author received a New Mexico Governor's Award in 1987

Subjects: Air pilots, Military, Ulibarrí, Sabine R., United States. Army Air Forces—Biography, World War, 1939-1945

Read-aloud excerpt: Pages 27 through 31

Booktalk: Sabine R. Ulibarrí grew up in the mountains of northern New Mexico. After graduating from high school, he attended the University of New Mexico until the death of his parents. Taking on the responsibility of caring for his four younger brothers and sisters, he left the university and taught for four years in public schools in New Mexico. In 1942 with World War II in progress, he went to Washington D.C. to attend a university and to work as a translator in a civil service job. Since he had dependents, he was exempt from the draft, but he soon returned home, married, and enlisted. His unique experiences in World War II are the focus of this memoir.

Related Titles:

Among the Valiant: Mexican Americans in WWII and Korea by Raul Morin. Borden
>	Publishing, 1963

Double Victory: A Multicultural History of America in World War II by Ronald Takaki. Little,
>	Brown, 2000

62. The Meaning of Consuelo

Author: **Judith Ortiz Cofer** is a Puerto Rican professor of English at the University of Georgia. The author of novels, essays, autobiographies, and poetry, Ortiz Cofer lives in Georgia. <www.english.uga.edu/~jcofer>

Publication: Farrar, Straus, and Giroux, 2003. 185 pages

Genre: Contemporary fiction   *Level:* Young Adult

Note: Américas Award Winner

Summary: As Consuelo, the serious child, and her younger sister Mili, the charming lighthearted daughter, grow up in Puerto Rico in the 1950's, things change in their country and in their lives.

Subjects: Coming of age, Loss (Psychology), Psychological fiction, Puerto Ricans—Fiction, Sisters

Read-aloud excerpt: Pages 12 through 13

Booktalk: Consuelo and Mili grew up in Puerto Rico in the 1950's. When the family moved to San Juan from a pueblo on the coast, life began to change. Their father embraced the modern changes and influence of the United States, but their mother cared more about nature and old Puerto Rico. Consuelo was the older daughter, serious, the dark sister. Her name meant consolation or comfort. Her sister Mili's name was short for Milagros, the Spanish word for miracles. Mili was a child of light, her parents' delight. Consuelo was expected to be Mili's protector, and she took her role very seriously. In time, Mili began to act strangely but for awhile the family ignored her increasingly bizarre behavior. As Consuelo's fifteenth birthday approached, her parents were so involved in their own troubled relationship and worry about Mili that no mention was made of this special birthday. More and more resentful of the effects of Mili's mental problems on all their lives, Consuelo decided to take charge of her own life, but the results of her actions on her birthday were much more far-reaching and troubling than she ever could have imagined.

Related Titles:

Poe Park by Agnes Martinez. Holiday House, 2004

63. Mismatch

Author: **Lensey Namioka** was born in China and immigrated to the United States when she was a child. Namioka, the author of a number of award-winning books, lives in Seattle. <www.lensey.com/home.html>

Publication: Delacorte Press, 2006. 217 pages

Genre: Contemporary fiction   *Level:* Young Adult

Note: Books for the Teen Age (NYPL)

Summary: Their families clash when a Japanese-American teenaged boy starts dating a Chinese-American teenaged girl.

Subjects: Chinese Americans—Fiction, Dating (Social customs), Family life—Fiction, High schools—Fiction, Interracial dating, Japanese Americans—Fiction, Schools—Fiction

Read-aloud excerpt: Pages 3 through 5

Booktalk: Sue Hua first saw Andy Suzuki at the auditions for the Lakeview High School orchestra. Both are musicians; Sue is a viola player, and Andy plays the violin. Sue's family recently moved to the suburbs from an area where there were many cultures. Now she is one of the few non-white students at her new high school. Andy and Sue notice each other immediately and want to get to know each other better. They are both Asian American. Perfect, right? Not exactly. Sue is Chinese American. Her grandmother has terrible frightening memories of a childhood in China when the Japanese invaded their country. Grandmother hates Japanese people. Andy is Japanese American. His parents are pretty tolerant of others, he thinks. However, when his father relates the bad experiences he had on a business trip to China, Andy realizes that his parents may not be as open-minded as he thought. How important is the history of their different cultures? Can Sue and Andy ever expect their families to understand, to accept them as a couple?

Related Titles:
Romiette and Julio by Sharon M. Draper. Atheneum, 1999

64. Name Me Nobody

Author: **Lois-Ann Yamanaka**, Japanese American, was born in Hawaii. The author of award-winning novels and poetry and a teacher, Yamanaka lives in Honolulu. <www.yamanakanaau.com/about_us.htm>

Publication: Hyperion, 1999. 229 pages

Genre: Contemporary fiction   *Level:* Young Adult

Note: Popular Paperbacks for Young Adults (ALA)

Summary: Emi-Lou struggles to come of age in her middle school years in Hawaii.

Subjects: Baseball—Fiction, Hawaii, Homosexuality, Schools—Fiction, Self-esteem—Fiction, Weight control

Read-aloud excerpt: Pages 49 through 51

Booktalk: Thirteen-year-old Japanese American Emi-Lou Kaya lives with her grandmother in Hawaii. Her mother Roxanne is never there for her only daughter, but Emi-Lou does have a protector, Yvonne, who calls herself Von. Von sticks up for Emi-Lou when the kids at school tease her about being fat. Every time Emi-Lou's mother disappoints her and life looks bad, Von is there for Emi-Lou to talk to. Always, that is, until Von meets Babes, another girl, and the two of them start spending lots of time together. Some people say Babes is a butchie, a lesbian, but Emi-Lou doesn't want to believe that because that would mean that Von is one also. Von helps Emi-Lou lose weight with diet pills and laxatives and sometimes Emi-Lou has to starve, but people start to look at her differently as she gets slimmer. Emi-Lou is interested in Kyle although she knows he is using her to do his classwork for him. Sterling seemed to like her, but if he really likes her, why does he keep hanging around with Viva? Why does Viva seem to think Sterling is hers?

Related Titles:

First Among Nisei: The Life and Writings of Masaji Maramoto by Dennis M. Ogawa. University of Hawaii, 2007

65. Naming Maya

Author: **Uma Krishnaswami** was born in India. The author of picture books and fiction, she published her first poem when she was thirteen. Krishnaswami lives in New Mexico. <www.umakrishnaswami.com>

Publication: Farrar Straus Giroux, 2004. 178 pages

Genre: Contemporary fiction   *Level:* Young Adult

Note: Notable Books for a Global Society

Summary: When Maya accompanies her mother to India, she uncovers family history relating to her parents' divorce and learns more about herself and her mother.

Subjects: Divorce, East Indian Americans—Fiction, Family life—Fiction, India, Mothers and daughters—Fiction

Read-aloud excerpt: Pages 3 through 6

Booktalk: When Maya and her mother go to India to sell Maya's grandfather's house, Mami, the old woman who was the cook and housekeeper before, returns and insists on taking up her old duties. Although Maya and her mother will be there only as long as it takes to sell the house, it soon becomes obvious that the old cook will be a part of Maya's life whether she is wanted or not. Maya's parents are divorced and Maya feels really bad about that. Even worse is the fact that her father does not seem to be interested in her and does not want to see his only daughter. Her mother is busy with the business of selling the house so Maya is often alone. How will she spend her time in this strange country that is not really her own? Will she make friends? Can the old cook help her understand why her parents divorced? Are there clues from the family's past in Mami's memory?

Related Titles:

Looking for Bapu by Anjali Banerjee. Wendy Lamb Books, 2006

66. Never Mind the Goldbergs

Author: **Matthue Roth**, a Jewish performance poet and writer, lives in San Francisco. <www.matthue.com>

Publication: PUSH/Scholastic, 2005. 362 pages

Genre: Contemporary fiction   *Level:* Young Adult

Note: Popular Paperbacks for Young Adults (ALA)

Summary: A seventeen-year-old Orthodox Jewish girl leaves her home in New York for the summer to film a television show in California.

Subjects: Jews—Fiction, New York—Fiction, Television programs

Read-aloud excerpt: Pages 2 through 3

Booktalk: It's the last day of classes of her junior year for Hava Aaronson, a seventeen-year-old Orthodox Jewish girl. Hava stands out from her peers in the all-girls private Jewish school. Her hair is streaked, purple and burgundy. She wears death rock T-shirts and not one, but several skirts of various lengths. After Hava is reprimanded for flipping through the pages of her textbook in Prophets class, she speaks disrespectfully to the teacher, Rabbi Greenberg. Of course, Hava is in trouble, big trouble, but that is nothing new for her. When she is called to Rabbi Greenberg's office from Yiddish class, she expects the worst. Instead, a voice of a movie producer on the phone offers Hava a spot in a new television sitcom about Jews. If she agrees, she will fly from New York to Los Angeles and spend the summer working on the show. She will be alone, without her parents, on her own in an apartment for the summer. Can she maintain her Orthodox Jewish identity in Hollywood? Will God approve or is she considering venturing into the realm of the forbidden?

Related Titles:

How to Ruin a Summer Vacation by Simone Elkeles. Flux, 2006
How to Ruin My Teenage Life by Simone Elkeles. Flux, 2007

67. Nilda: A Novel

Author: **Nicholasa Mohr** was born in New York after her parents came to the mainland from Puerto Rico. She is an artist and the author of thirteen books. <www.ualr.edu/teenread/id24.htm>

Publication: Harper & Row, 1973; Arte Público Press, 1986. 292 pages

Genre: Historical fiction   *Level:* Young Adult

Note: James Addams Children's Book Award

Summary: A girl growing up in Spanish Harlem in the 1940's watches the secure world of her childhood years slowly erode.

Subjects: New York—Fiction, Puerto Ricans—Fiction

Read-aloud excerpt: Pages 51 through 54

Booktalk: Nilda Ramirez, ten years old in 1941, lived with her Puerto Rican family in New York. That summer Nilda went to a Catholic camp in New Jersey to escape the city heat. The camp was a horrible place where the children had to clean their plates although the food was awful. There was no hot water in the showers. The toilet stalls didn't have doors, and everyone had to take a dose of laxative each night. When the plumbing failed and the children were sent home, things were not good at Nilda's home either. Her stepfather was sick and could not work. Nilda's brother Jimmy got mixed up with drugs and his Russian girlfriend got kicked out of her mother's house. When Pearl Harbor was bombed, Nilda's brothers Paul and Victor could not wait to join the military. Can Nilda deal with all the trouble in her life and the ugly, blatant prejudice from policemen and teachers at school?

Related Titles:

El Bronx Remembered: A Novella and Stories by Nicholasa Mohr. Harper & Row, 1975; Arte Público Press, 1986

68. Nobody's Son: Notes from an American Life

Author: **Luis Alberto Urrea** is of mixed descent. His father was Mexican and his mother American. An author of nonfiction, fiction, and poetry, Urrea is a professor at a university in Illinois. <www.luisurrea.com/home.php>

Publication: University of Arizona Press, 1998. 188 pages

Genre: Memoir   *Level:* Adult

Note: American Book Award

Subjects: Authors, American—Biography, Mexican Americans—Biography, Urrea, Luis Alberto

Read-aloud excerpt: Pages 57 through 59

Booktalk: I am Luis Alberto Urrea. Like William Carlos Williams, I am a poet. Like him, I am Latino. Half-breeds both, he and I. My mother was white. My father was Mexican. To my mother I was Louis. To my father I was Luis. Am I Latino? Mexican American? Chicano? Hispanic? Mexican? My mother hated Mexicans. Did that hatred include me? Who am I? My mother's son? My father's? In this memoir I write about my life, about life along the border, about language, disease, memories good and bad, violence, machismo and sex, religion, love and hate, ugliness and beauty, Mexico and the United States, all a part of my American life.

Related Titles:

Capirotada: A Nogales Memoir by Alberto Alvaro Ríos. University of New Mexico Press, 1999

Mayan Drifter: Chicano Poet in the Lowlands of America by Juan Felipe Herrera. Temple University Press, 1997

A Place to Stand: The Making of a Poet by Jimmy Santiago Baca. Grove Press, 2001

Working in the Dark by Jimmy Santiago Baca. Red Crane Books, 1991

69. The Not-So-Star-Spangled Life of Sunita Sen: A Novel

Author: **Mitali Perkins**, born in India, lived with her family in Ghana, London, New York, and Mexico before settling in California when Mitali was in middle school. A teacher and author, she lives in Massachusetts. <www.mitaliperkins.com>

Publication: Little, Brown, 2005. 176 pages

Genre: Contemporary fiction   *Level:* Young Adult

Note: Books for the Teen Age (NYPL), Lamplighter Award

Summary: When her grandparents come for a visit from India, Sunita finds herself resenting her Indian heritage and embarrassed by differences between her and her friends.

Subjects: California—Fiction, East Indian Americans—Fiction, Family life—Fiction, Friendship, Grandparents

Read-aloud excerpt: Pages 7 through 10

Booktalk: Sunita Sen is thirteen and is not allowed to wear makeup, not even lipstick, even though almost every other girl in the eighth grade can. Her friendship with Michael Morrison probably will not survive for much longer because Sunita's grandparents arrived from India last week. Everything has changed. Sunita's mother has stopped being her mother and has become a daughter to her parents. She has taken leave from her job to stay home and be a good Indian wife, has switched from business suits to traditional Indian clothing, and even wears a red dot in the middle of her forehead. The grandparents have taken Sunita's room so she must share a room with her sister. Instead of pizza and takeout, they now eat traditional Indian foods. It is embarrassing to have grandparents who look and think like they do. She is not allowed to have boys come to the house now. It is all too weird, and their visit is going to last a year! Soon Sunita starts to feel strange about herself and her family and worries about how her friends will react to her grandparents. She loves them, but they are so Indian! It just is not fair that everybody's American lives have to change just because they are visiting.

Related Titles:

First Daughter: Extreme American Makeover by Mitali Perkins. Dutton, 2007

70. Nothing but the Truth (and a few white lies)

Author: **Justina Chen Headley**, Taiwanese American, grew up in New York and California, worked as a magazine editor in Australia, and now lives in the Pacific Northwest where she is a full-time writer. <www.justinachenheadley.com>

Publication: Little, Brown, 2006. 241 pages

Genre: Contemporary fiction   *Level:* Young Adult

Note: Asian Pacific American Award Winner

Summary: Fifteen-year-old Patty Ho, half-Taiwanese and half-white, never fits in until her mother ships her off to math camp where she becomes comfortable with her true self.

Subjects: Mothers and daughters—Fiction, Prejudices, Racially mixed people—Fiction, Self-esteem—Fiction, Single-parent families—Fiction, Stanford University, Taiwanese Americans—Fiction

Read-aloud excerpt: Pages 117 through 118

Booktalk: Fifteen-year-old Patty Ho is hapa, half-Taiwanese and half-white, but she wishes she were all white. On the night of the spring fling when the other kids are dancing the night away, Patty is having her future read by an old lady who examines her belly button. Patty's older brother Abe's future is already determined. He will be going to Harvard in the fall. Their mother is thrilled about that, but she is not pleased by the fortune teller's assessment of Patty's future. Soon her mother announces that Patty will be going to math summer camp at Stanford. Patty knows the only reason her mother wants her to go is to keep her from dating and especially from dating a white guy. Patty and Abe's dad was a white guy, but he has been out of their lives for a long time. Patty had a crush on a white guy at school until he sat silently by when Steve Kosanko called her a half-breed and spat in her face. After that humiliation from an Asian guy, Patty begins to think maybe math camp is not such a bad idea after all. Of course she would not dream of letting her mother know that.

Related Titles:

Girl Overboard by Justina Chen Headley. Little, Brown, 2008

71. Our House on Hueco

Author: **Carlos Nicolas Flores** is a Mexican American author of a novel and short stories. Flores teaches at a college and is a founder and co-director of the South Texas Writing Project in Laredo, Texas.
<www.ttup.ttu.edu/BookPages/0896725731.html>

Publication: Texas Tech University Press, 2006. 234 pages

Genre: Contemporary fiction   *Level:* Young Adult

Note: Premio Aztlan nominee, Tomas Rivera Award nominee

Summary: Junior and his family move from the barrio to a better part of El Paso, but they live in the basement of the new house as they try to raise their standard of living.

Subjects: El Paso, Texas, Family life—Fiction, Mexican Americans—Fiction, Texas—Fiction

Read-aloud excerpt: Pages 2 through 5

Booktalk: Junior was ten when his father bought a house on Hueco Street. Junior's father was Puerto Rican, and his mother, Mexican. Pop was excited when he took them to see their new house because now they could move out of a small apartment into a nice house with trees and a yard in a good neighborhood. Pop was full of plans to build an apartment in the back yard. Excitement turned to confusion when two gringo kids walked out of the front door of the house. Why were those Americanos in the new house? Then Pop revealed his plan. He had rented the house to the family of a sergeant at the nearby army base. Junior's family would live in the basement. In this way they would invest in their future, Pop said. The basement did not have a bathroom and it was dark and dirty. Could they really live there? Would Mom be able to accept the sergeant's wife who wore shorts and had a figure that made men look a little too long? Would Pop's plan work or would Mom and the boys move to Mexico to live with their grandmother? Could Junior and his brother Rafa possibly become friends with the gringo kids upstairs? Would the house on Hueco ever be truly theirs?

Related Titles:
The Other Side of the Tracks: A Novel by Tony Cano. Reata Press, 2001

72. Out of the Shadows: An Artist's Journey

Author: **Neil Waldman**, a Jewish American artist and writer who has illustrated more than thirty books, lives in New York State.
<http://artsnet.net/waldman/index.htm>

Publication: Boyds Mills Press, 2006. 144 pages

Genre: Memoir   *Level:* Young Adult

Subjects: Artists—Biography, Jews—Biography, Waldman, Neil

Read-aloud excerpt: Pages 65 through 68

Booktalk: Neil Waldman began drawing and painting to escape. The oldest son of Jewish parents, he grew up in New York City. Because of his parents' troubled marriage, Neil and his brother and sister were often witnesses to their parents' arguments, but his grandparents and extended family provided love and support and helped give Neil an understanding of culture, both their rich Jewish culture and the artistic culture of the city. This is the story of how Neil Waldman overcame the negativity of his awful childhood, began recording his feelings in a journal, and, with the help of Vincent Van Gogh, became a painter and illustrator, a writer, and a teacher.

Related Titles:
In Jewish Texas by Stanley E. Ely. Texas Christian University Press, 1998
Yom Kippur a Go-Go by Matthue Roth. Cleis Press, 2005

73. Parrot in the Oven: Mi vida: A Novel

Author: **Victor Martinez**, a Mexican American California native, worked as a driver, firefighter, clerk, field worker, and teacher. Author of poems, essays, and stories, he lives in California.
<www.harpercollins.com/authors/12450/Victor_Martinez/index.aspx>

Publication: HarperCollins Publishers, 1996. 216 pages

Genre: Contemporary fiction   *Level:* Young Adult

Note: Américas Award Winner, Pura Belpré Award Winner, National Book Award

Summary: Manny relates his coming of age experiences as a member of a poor Mexican American family in which the alcoholic father only adds to everyone's struggle.

Subjects: Alcoholism, Family life—Fiction, Mexican Americans—Fiction

Read-aloud excerpt: Pages 71 through 74

Booktalk: Manny's dad lost his job as interpreter for the city because he drank beer during lunch too many times. Then there isn't any money coming in to buy groceries or pay the bills. Manny is a smart kid with good grades. His mother wants him to go to a better school across town that offers more opportunities. He needs money to buy clothes and school supplies and he really wants a baseball mitt. He and his brother Nardo try field work, picking chili peppers, but that does not earn them much money for all their hard work. When a kind teacher gives him twenty dollars after he sees Manny's pathetic hand-me-down shoes, Dad takes the money and goes on a two-day drunk. When Mom goes to the pool hall to bring her husband home, Dad's pride is hurt. In a drunken rage he gets out his twenty-two rifle and starts searching for the bullets he knows are hidden somewhere. He is going to teach his wife's friend Sophie a lesson.

Related Titles:
Drift by Manuel Luis Martinez. Picador, 2003

74. Plain City

Author: **Virginia Hamilton**, African American, was born in Ohio, granddaughter of a slave. Her heritage included African and Native American ancestors. Married to Arnold Adoff, she died in February 2002.

Publication: Blue Sky Press, 1993. 194 pages

Genre: Contemporary fiction　　*Level:* Young Adult

Summary: Twelve-year-old Buhlaire, a "mixed" child feels out of place in her community, struggles to unearth her past, her family history, and her long-missing father.

Subjects: African Americans—Fiction, Fathers and daughters, Identity, Racially mixed people—Fiction

Read-aloud excerpt: Pages 19 through 20

Booktalk: Buhlaire Sims' hair is straw-colored, worn in Rasta twists. Her eyes are gray or blue-green, depending on the light, and her skin is a mixture of honey and carrot tones. She lives with her aunts in a Water House, a house on stilts beside the river. Buhlair gets teased a lot because of where she lives and because she looks different. Buhlaire's mother is singer and dancer, Bluezy Sims, who makes an occasional appearance at home but is often on the road working. Buhlaire's father, the late Theodore 'Junior' Sims, is dead, a victim of the Vietnam War. At least that is what Buhlaire has figured out from the available facts. Her daddy must have been a war hero, died a soldier in that war. At school Grady keeps following Buhlair and making fun of her until one day in the cafeteria, Buhlaire has had enough. More than enough. She marches over to Grady, grabs his mouth and pours chocolate milk into it and down his face. Revenge! Perfect! Of course, it does not end there. Buhlaire gets sent to the principal's office, and what she learns there changes her life forever.

Related Titles:

I Wanna Be Your Shoebox by Cristina García. Simon & Schuster, 2008

Off-Color by Janet McDonald. Farrar, Straus and Giroux, 2007

The Window by Michael Dorris. Hyperion Books for Children, 1997

75. Power

Author: Linda Hogan, Chickasaw, grew up in a military family and spent much of her childhood in Oklahoma and Colorado. Hogan, a university professor and author of poetry, novels, and essays, writes full-time.
<www.nativewiki.org/Linda_Hogan>

Publication: W. W. Norton, 1998. 235 pages

Genre: Contemporary fiction   **Level:** Adult

Note: Author received Lifetime Achievement Award from Native Writers' Circle

Summary: Sixteen-year-old Omishto sees Aunt Ama kill an endangered panther, an animal that is sacred to her Taiga people.

Subjects: Florida—Fiction, Indians of North America—Fiction, Mothers and daughters—Fiction, Panther

Read-aloud excerpt: Pages 105 through 108

Booktalk: Sixteen-year-old Omishto is Taiga, one of the ancient swamp people in what is now called Florida. She is one of thirty Taiga left in this world. Her name means One Who Watches. Omishto lives with her mother, stepfather, and sister. Her stepfather looks at her in evil ways so that she knows what he is thinking, what he wants to do to her. At school Omishto is a good student, a model for other Indian kids, an Indian girl with potential, a shining exception. That is how the teachers see her. Omishto goes often to visit Aunt Ama, an independent Taiga woman who lives alone keeping the old traditions. In the devastation following a hurricane, Omishto goes with Ama on a hunt. At first, Omishto thinks they are hunting for a wounded deer, but instead they find a pathetic half-starved panther. When Ama kills the panther, an endangered species, both Ama and Omishto know that trouble will follow because a federal law has been broken. Ama is taken away by the authorities and Omishto, who has lost her friend and place of refuge, her link to the old ways, must go on alone.

Related Titles:

Mean Spirit by Linda Hogan. Atheneum, 1990

Solar Storms by Linda Hogan. Scribner, 1995

76. Quesadilla Moon

Author: **Gary D. Castillo**, a Mexican American native of California, worked as a music professor in Los Angeles and is now a teacher in California. *Quesadilla Moon* is Castillo's first book.
<www.arte.uh.edu/view_book.aspx?isbn=1558854339>

Publication: Piñata Books, 2007. 100 pages

Genre: Contemporary fiction   *Level:* Young Adult

Summary: David, a migrant worker, loves to sing but his father does not approve. When he sees an opportunity to sing at a church competition, David decides to try out.

Subjects: African Americans—Fiction, Fathers and sons, Mexican Americans—Fiction, Migrant agricultural workers—Fiction

Read-aloud excerpt: Pages 9 through 11

Booktalk: David Dominguez and his family were migrant farm workers. David always loved to sing, but his father believed that singing was for sissies. Once the owner of a grocery store gave David a loaf of bread in return for singing a song. Later he gathered an audience who gave him coins because they liked his singing, but his father was very angry when he discovered what David was doing. For a while David attended the African American Living Faith Apostolic Church because he loved the music there. David's family was Catholic and he was not African American, but he became friends with church member Sister Mae, who told David that he had the "gift." Sister Mae gave him voice lessons, but that ended when his family moved. By the time he was a teenager, David had given up his dream of a musical career. Then a whirlwind miraculously brought him information about a singing contest at the Four Square Apostolic Church. Should he try out? What could it hurt? Maybe no one from his family would ever know.

Related Titles:
Under the Feet of Jesus by Helena María Viramontes. Dutton, 1995

77. Rain Is Not My Indian Name

Author: **Cynthia Leitich Smith**, a mixed blood, enrolled member of the Muscogee (Creek) Nation, grew up in Kansas and now lives in Austin, Texas, with her husband Greg Leitich Smith, a lawyer and writer. <www.cynthialeitichsmith.com>

Publication: HarperCollins, 2001. 135 pages

Genre: Contemporary fiction   *Level:* Young Adult

Summary: Tired of staying in seclusion since the death of her best friend, a four-teen-year-old Native American girl takes on a photographic assignment with her local newspaper to cover events at the Native American summer youth camp.

Subjects: Death, Grief, Indians of North America—Fiction, Photography—Fiction

Read-aloud excerpt: Pages 113 through 116

Booktalk: Cassidy Rain Berghoff lives in the small town of Hannesburg, Kansas, with her grandfather and her older brother while her father works in Guam. Her mother died six years ago after being struck by lightning. Rain inherited Muscogee Creek, Cherokee, and Scots Irish blood from her mother. From her father's side of the family tree, her heritage is Irish, German, and Ojibway. She is a "mixed blood." More important, however, she is a fourteen-year-old girl who enjoys photography and worries because she has never been kissed by a boy. On New Year's Day, her birthday, she and her longtime friend Galen have their first date, a date that changes Rain's life forever.

Related Titles:

Tantalize by Cynthia Leitich Smith. Candlewick Press, 2007

78. Rebel without a Crew or, How a 23-Year-Old Filmmaker with $7,000 Became a Hollywood Player

Author: **Robert Rodriguez,** a Mexican American Hollywood filmmaker, grew up in Texas. <www.tribute.ca/people/Robert+Rodriguez/5086>

Publication: Dutton, 1995. 285 pages

Genre: Memoir   *Level:* Adult

Subjects: Mariachi (Motion picture), Mexican Americans—Biography, Motion picture producers and directors, Rodriguez, Robert, 1968

Read-aloud excerpt: Pages x through xiv

Booktalk: My name is Robert Rodriguez. You may have heard of some of my films. *El Mariachi* and *Desperado* are two of the early ones. This book is sort of a combination of a memoir and a how-to manual. The first part of the book contains excerpts from the journal that I kept starting in March 1991 and continuing through February 1993. Those journal entries reflect how I came to produce *El Mariachi*, my first feature film. If you are really interested in being a filmmaker, you will want to read the appendix, "The Ten-Minute Film School." Any of you would-be writers who are interested in drama or film might want to read the other appendix, the original screenplay of *El Mariachi*. Those of you who are not really that interested in film might be interested in this book because it reflects my philosophy: if you really want something, be willing to do what it takes as long as it takes without giving up. That is the secret of my success.

Related Titles:
Grindhouse: The Sleaze-filled Saga of an Exploitation Double Feature by Quentin Tarantino and Robert Rodriguez. Weinstein Books, 2007

79. Sammy & Juliana in Hollywood

Author: **Benjamin Alire Sáenz**, Mexican American, was born and grew up in New Mexico. Sáenz studied philosophy and theology in Europe and traveled before becoming a writer and a university professor in El Paso, Texas. <http://www.benjaminaliresaenz.com/>

Publication: HarperTempest, 2006. 291 pages

Genre: Contemporary fiction   **Level:** Young Adult

Note: Américas Award nominee, *LA Times* Book Prize, YALSA Best Books

Summary: As a Chicano boy in the unglamorous town of Hollywood, New Mexico, and a member of the graduating class of 1969, Sammy Santos faces the challenges of "gringo" racism, unpopular dress codes, the Vietnam War, barrio violence, and poverty.

Subjects: Death, Grief, Mexican Americans—Fiction, Poverty, Violence

Read-aloud excerpt: Pages 114 through 116

Booktalk: In 1968 Sammy Santos lives in Hollywood, the Mexican barrio of Las Cruces, New Mexico. Sammy is a good boy who works hard to please his father, is good to his little sister Elena, and is respectful to Mrs. Apodaca, the neighbor who criticizes every-thing about him. Sammy tries to be a good Catholic in spite of the Irish priest who hates Sammy and his people. Sammy's friends call Sammy *the Librarian*, among other things, because of his determination to do well in school, to go to college, and to get out of Hollywood. Sammy loves Juliana, but none of the adults in his life approve of her because of her family. The war that isn't called a war is taking boys to Vietnam. Drug overdoses are becoming commonplace in the barrio. Some parents abuse their children without any consequences. Most of the school's teachers and administrators are small-minded bigots. Tragedy strikes again and again during Sammy's senior year. Will he and his friends of the class of 1969 be victims or victorious?

Related Titles:
Fallen Angels by Walter Dean Myers. Scholastic, 1988

80. The Secret of Dead Man's Mine: A Rinnah Two Feathers Mystery

Author: **Rodney Johnson**, of Lakota Sioux heritage, grew up in South Dakota. The author of a series of mysteries for young readers, Johnson lives in Los Angeles.

Publication: UglyTown, 2001. 241 pages

Genre: Contemporary fiction   *Level:* Young Adult

Summary: Rinnah Two Feathers, a sleuth-minded Lakota Indian, investigates a stranger poking around an abandoned house and stumbles across the secret of Dead Man's Mine.

Subjects: Indians of North American—Fiction, Mystery and detective stories, North Dakota, Teton Indians—Fiction

Read-aloud excerpt: Pages 22 through 23

Booktalk: It is almost the end of the school year for Rinnah Two Feathers, a Lakota Indian who lives with her mother who owns and operates Circle Feather Lodge, a guest house on the Rosebud Reservation. One morning while riding on the school bus with her friend Tommy Red Hawk and the obnoxious Victor Little Horn and his two friends, Rinnah is intrigued when she sees a tall man in a black raincoat and cowboy hat walking around an abandoned house beside the road. Who is he? What is he doing there? What is that metal box he took out of an unusual bag that looked like it had been made from an old rug? Soon strange things start happening all over the place. Tommy's dad is attacked at the museum where he works. A guest at the lodge has her rolls of camera film stolen. Why are all these weird things happening? Meagen Paige, a new girl at school, joins Rinnah and Tommy as they seek answers to these and other mysteries.

Related Titles:
The Curse of the Royal Ruby: A Rinnah Two Feathers Mystery by Rodney Johnson. UglyTown, 2002

81. Seeing Emily

Author: **Joyce Lee Wong**, Chinese American, is a graduate of the University of Virginia School of Law. Wong has been a lawyer and a teacher and now lives in Los Angeles. *Seeing Emily* is her first published book.

Publication: Amulet Books, 2005. 268 pages.

Genre: Contemporary fiction   *Level:* Young Adult

Note: Author received Promising New Poet Award, Lee Bennett Hopkins Poetry Award

Summary: The author relates in free verse the experiences of Emily, an artist and daughter of immigrants, who tries to reconcile her American self and her Chinese heritage.

Subjects: Artists—Fiction, Chinese Americans—Fiction, Family life—Fiction, High schools—Fiction, Schools—Fiction, Self-perception

Read-aloud excerpt: Pages 244 through 246

Booktalk: Sophomore Emily Wu works with her parents at their restaurant, Golden Palace, most week nights. Emily tries to be a good daughter. She studies hard to make good grades and usually does what her parents tell her. Sometimes though, like when her mother wants her to call Alex Huang, the son of Emily's mother's college classmate, Emily resents her mother trying to run her life. Alex is a new student at her school, but Emily is more interested in getting the attention of Nick, an older non-Chinese boy instead. After they start working on a mural at school, Emily and Alex become casual friends. Then Nick and Emily begin dating. She likes Nick a lot, but sometimes it seems as though he is dating her just because she is Chinese American, because she is exotic, rather than seeing her as a real person. Then she has a chance to go to Taipei for the summer to learn Chinese. Should she go? What about Nick? What about her friends Nina and Liz? And what about Alex?

Related Titles:
The Kitchen God's Wife by Amy Tan. Putnam, 1991
Mona in the Promised Land by Gish Jen. Knopf, 1991

82. The Singing Mountain

Author: **Sonia Levitin** is Jewish. She was born in Germany and moved with her family to the United States when she was a young child. A university teacher and the author of more than forty books, she lives in California.
<www.sonialevitin.com/bio.html>

Publication: Simon & Schuster Books for Young Readers, 1998. 261 pages

Genre: Contemporary fiction   *Level:* Young Adult

Note: Sydney Taylor Award Honor Book

Summary: While traveling in Israel for the summer, Mitch decides to stay and pursue a life of Jewish orthodoxy, forcing him to make decisions about family and life.

Subjects: California—Fiction, Cousins, Family life—Fiction, Israel, Jews—Fiction

Read-aloud excerpt: Pages 15 through 17

Booktalk: During the summer after high school graduation, Mitch Green goes on a trip to Israel. His parents and his cousin Carlie, who has lived with them since her parents' death, are expecting him to return to California soon, where he will get

ready to attend college. When a telephone call informs them that Mitch has disappeared, everyone is naturally worried. When he reappears but refuses to come home
with the other travelers, his parents are concerned and upset. Carlie is caught in the
middle. She does not know how she feels. There are so many unanswered questions. Why is Mitch staying there? Is he being influenced by some ultra religious
Jewish cult? Are they after his money? Their family is Jewish, but they don't take
their religion to extremes. Years ago before their family name was Green it was
Greenberg. Members of the family were involved in the Holocaust, but that is
ancient history that no one talks about now. What is holding Mitch in Israel?

Related Titles:

Strange Relations by Sonia Levitin. Alfred A. Knopf, 2007

83. *Spared Angola: Memories from a Cuban-American Childhood*

Author: **Virgil Suárez** was born in Cuba. With his parents he went to Spain and
then to the United States. The author of several published works of fiction, Suárez
is a teacher of creative writing at Florida State University.
<http://english.fsu.edu/faculty/vsuarez.htm>

Publication: Arte Público Press, 1997. 159 pages

Genre: Memoir   *Level:* Adult

Subjects: Cuban Americans—Biography, Suárez, Virgil, 1962-

Read-aloud excerpt: Pages 95 through 96

Booktalk: Virgil Suárez was born in Havana, Cuba, in 1962. An only child, he spent
the first years of his life surrounded by family and friends in Fidel Castro's post-
revolutionary communist Cuba. Virgil and his family were called gusanos, worms,
because his parents were considered counter-revolutionaries or dissidents. They had
applied for permits to leave the country because they did not want their son to be
conscripted into military service in Angola. Eventually the family was allowed to
go to Spain. There they lived for four years before moving to Los Angeles,
California, where Virgil attended school, learned English, and was inspired to
become a writer and a teacher.

Related Titles:

Going Under by Virgil Suarez. Arte Público Press, 1996

84. Tae's Sonata

Author: **Haemi Balgassi**, Korean American, emigrated from Seoul, Korea as a child. A writer, editor, and teacher, Balgassi lives in New England. <www.haemibalgassi.com>

Publication: Clarion Books, 1997. 123 pages

Genre: Contemporary fiction   *Level:* Young Adult

Note: Lamplighter Award, American Booksellers Pick of the Lists, NCSS/CBC Notable

Summary: Tae, a Korean American, tries to sort out her feelings when she is assigned a popular boy as a partner for a school report and has a falling out with her best friend.

Subjects: Friendship, Korean Americans—Fiction, Schools—Fiction

Read-aloud excerpt: Pages 13 through 15

Booktalk: Taeyoung Kim is dismayed when Mr. Babbett pairs her with Josh Morgan to do a report on South Korea. Why did he have to assign them South Korea? Did he do that because her family is Korean? Tae would certainly have preferred a non-Asian country like Canada or Spain. And why did their teacher put her with Josh, of all people? Josh is one of the Royals, snobby insiders that all hang around together. He should have been paired with Krista or Paige, girl Royals who are always laughing scornfully at Tae and the other outsiders. Josh seems nice enough, but Tae can just imagine him laughing at her family's shabby apartment and her mother's heavily-accented English. Thank goodness Tae has Megan, a true friend who is always there to listen. Philip Park, the only other Korean American in their class, may actually like her too. Rumors start to fly. Someone said that Tae had a crush on Josh. Then someone said they had heard that Josh asked to be paired with Tae because he needed to make a good grade in that class. Will Josh and Tae be able to work together on this project? Maybe everything will work out . . . or not.

Related Titles:
Stella: On the Edge of Popularity by Lauren Lee. Polychrome, 1994

85. Teen Angel

Author: **Gloria L. Velásquez**, Mexican American, grew up in Colorado. A poet, musician, and novelist, Velásquez is a professor at California Polytechnic State University in San Luis Obispo, California. <http://cla.calpoly.edu/~gvelasqu/main.html>

Publication: Piñata Books, 2003. 154 pages

Genre: Contemporary fiction   *Level:* Young Adult

Note: Roosevelt High School series

Summary: When fifteen-year-old Celia Chávez becomes pregnant, she receives help from her friends, family, and a psychiatrist who recently had a miscarriage.

Subjects: Family life—Fiction, Mexican Americans—Fiction, Pregnancy

Read-aloud excerpt: Pages 53 through 56

Booktalk: Celia Chávez is fifteen years old. She likes to wear short skirts and clothes that show off her figure. Her old-fashioned father will not let her date yet, and she may never get to date because her sister Juanita is older and she still is not allowed to date. When Celia meets her friend Cassie's cousin from Chicago, she can tell that Nicky likes her looks as much as she likes his. Cassie is not all that crazy about her snobbish cousin, but when he asks Celia to meet him at Lakeside Park, she finds a way to sneak out without her father getting suspicious. At that first meeting Nicky kisses her, the first time she has ever been kissed by a boy. Then Celia knows that she is in love. She cannot wait to be with him again. Even though she knows her father will kill her if he finds out she is secretly meeting a boy, Celia decides to take that risk when Nicky wants to meet her again. This time she arranges to spend the night with Cassie so she and Nicky can have more time together. They drive to Coral Beach where they sit on a blanket on the sand beside the ocean. He calls her an angel. He says that he loves her and wants to show her how much he loves her. After that night Celia's life will never be the same.

Related Titles:

Laura's Secret by Irma García. Chusma House, 1997

86. *The Tequila Worm*

Author: **Viola Canales**, Mexican American, grew up in Texas. Her experience includes being a captain in the U.S. Army, community organizer, lawyer, administrator in the U.S. Small Business Administration, and vice president of a corporation. She lives in California.
<www.randomhouse.com/kids/catalog/display.pperl?isbn=9780385746748>

Publication: Wendy Lamb Books, 2005. 199 pages

Genre: Contemporary fiction   *Level:* Young Adult

Note: Pura Belpre Award Winner, ALA Notable, Pen Center USA Award

Summary: Sofia, from a close-knit community in McAllen, Texas, finds that her experiences as a scholarship student at an Episcopal boarding school strengthen her ties to family and "comadres."

Subjects: Boarding schools—Fiction, Catholics—Fiction, Family life—Fiction,

Mexican Americans—Fiction, Neighborhood, Schools—Fiction, Texas—Fiction

Read-aloud excerpt: Pages 36 through 40

Booktalk: Growing up in a South Texas neighborhood, Sofia learns about her Mexican-American culture through daily life. As a little girl sitting on the front porch listening to Doña Clara's stories, she is told that she has the gift of "mule-kicking." In time she comes to understand that this ability to kick aside obstacles is a part of her destiny. When she is in the ninth grade, Sofia is given the chance to earn a scholarship to attend a fancy boarding school more than three hundred miles away. It is a wonderful opportunity, but she will have to leave her family, friends, the comfort of those early years. Her family is poor in terms of material things. Can she get the money she needs? What about the dresses that she will have to wear for the formal sit-down dinners at the school? Will the wealthy students at the new school accept her? Can she bear to be away from her father, mother, sister, and friends? If she does go, will she be making the biggest mistake of her life? Will the worm from a bottle of tequila help her?

Related Titles:
Caramelo by Sandra Cisneros. Vintage, 2003
Loving Pedro Infante by Denise Chavez. Washington Square Press, 2002

87. The Throwaway Piece

Author: **Jo Ann Yolanda Hernández**, Mexican American, has published two novels as well as fiction in journals. Hernández lives in Arizona.
<www.arte.uh.edu/view_book.aspx?isbn=1558853537>

Publication: Piñata Books, 2006. 246 pages

Genre: Contemporary fiction   *Level:* Young Adult

Summary: After entering the foster care system, Jewel takes care of her mother and, shutting herself off from others, is unaware of the influence she has on those around her.

Subjects: Abused women, Child abuse, Foster children—Fiction, Mothers and daughters, Self-esteem—Fiction

Read-aloud excerpt: Pages 8 through 11

Booktalk: Jewel's early years are spent with her mother, who goes from one man to another to another. It seems that she always picks the wrong man, always a man who hurts her. During those years Jewel is also badly hurt by several men, but after a while Jewel becomes her mother's protector. She takes care of her mother as much as she can. Then one horrible day, Jewel comes home to find a strange woman in their house. The woman is a social worker. Jewel's mother has had to make a decision. She had to choose between her latest boyfriend and her troublesome daughter. She chose the boyfriend. Jewel's suitcase is already packed and ready for her move into foster care. On that day Jewel became a State Kid, living in one foster home after another until she messed up enough to be removed and moved, again and again. Will she ever have friends? Is there an adult anywhere who will see past Jewel's outer shell and help her? Does she have a chance to ever be anything more than a State Kid?

Related Titles:

Luna's California Poppies by Alma Luz Villanueva. Bilingual Press/Editorial Bilingüe, 2002

88. The Treasure in the Tiny Blue Tin

Author: **Dede Fox Ducharme**, is a native of Texas and granddaughter of Jewish immigrants. Ducharme is a teacher and school librarian.

<www.scbwi-houston.org/Pages/ducharme.htm>

Publication: Texas Christian University Press, 1998. 144 pages

Genre: Historical fiction   *Level:* Young Adult

Note: Sydney Taylor Award Winner

Summary: In the early 1900's in Texas, a twelve-year-old Jewish immigrant searches for his father who he fears is sick, and is joined on his journey by a prejudiced country boy.

Subjects: Antisemitism—Fiction, Immigrants—Fiction, Jews—Fiction, Prejudices, Texas—Fiction

Read-aloud excerpt: Pages 7 through 9

Booktalk: In 1913 twelve-year-old Max Miller, born Muttel Mendelsohn, along with his father, mother, and a sister have immigrated to Texas. They live in Houston where Uncle Benny has a store. Max is in third grade and is learning English and making rapid progress while his peddler father travels the countryside selling his wares. When Papa does not come home for their first Passover celebration in America, Max fears that he is ill. Not wanting to alarm his mother, Max takes the new bike that his uncle has bought for grocery deliveries, packs something very special in a little tin box, and sets out to find Papa. He plans to make the trip alone but finds himself accompanied by Joe, a prejudiced boy whose father calls Max a dirty Jew. Certainly Max has enough trouble without having to deal with this kind of company!

Related Titles:

Lone Stars of David: The Jews of Texas edited by Hollace Ava Weiner and Kenneth D. Roseman. Brandeis University Press, 2007

89. Trino's Time

Author: **Diane Gonzales Bertrand** is a Mexican American native of Texas. The author of numerous award-winning books for children and young adults, she teaches writing at a university in San Antonio, Texas.
<www.arte.uh.edu/view_book_creator.aspx?CreatorID=46>

Publication: Piñata Books, 2001.171 pages

Genre: Contemporary fiction   *Level:* Young Adult

Note: Books for the Teen Age (NYPL), Tomás Rivera Award finalist

Summary: With the help of some friends and a Tejano hero that he discovers in history class, thirteen-year-old Trino copes with his problems and his world.

Subjects: Death, Family life—Fiction, Friendship, Mexican Americans—Fiction, Poverty, Schools—Fiction, Self-realization

Read-aloud excerpt: Pages 14 through 17

Booktalk: Trino Olivares lives with his mother and three younger brothers in a not-very-nice trailer. Money is scarce because his mom does not make much at her cleaning jobs, but she is too embarrassed by her lack of education to try for a better job at a nearby college. When Trino works with his mom's friend Nick cutting down trees, his mom expects him to give her every cent he makes. He knows that she needs the money to feed him and the other kids but still it does not seem fair. Trino starts working for old Mr. Epifaño at his grocery store after school partly because he feels guilty about being a witness to the robbery and beating of the old man and not telling anyone about what he saw. Trino took the wise course to save his own skin, but he does feel guilty about keeping quiet. He decides to keep this new part-time job a secret so he can have a little spending money. At school their social studies teacher gives them an assignment that requires research on José Antonio Navarro, a signer of the Texas Declaration of Independence. A problem develops when Hector, his research partner, says something insulting about Trino's mother. And that is just the beginning of Trino's troubles.

Related Titles:
Trino's Choice by Diane Gonzales Bertrand. Piñata Books, 1999

90. Two Badges: The Lives of Mona Ruiz

Author: **Mona Ruiz** with **Geoff Boucher** Mona Ruiz is Mexican American, a native of Santa Ana, California. She grew up there, attended school, and was involved in gangs before becoming a police officer. Geoff Boucher is a reporter and writer, coauthor of several books. <www.police-writers.com/mona_ruiz.html>

Publication: Arte Público Press, 1997. 288 pages

Genre: Memoir   *Level:* Adult

Subjects: Gangs—Biography, Law enforcement, Mexican Americans—Biography, Policewomen—Biography, Ruiz, Mona

Read-aloud excerpt: Pages 9 through 11

Booktalk: My name is Mona Ruiz. I was born Ramona Sandoval in Santa Ana, California in 1959, the second of eight children. When I was four, my father told me that the police were soldiers doing God's work on this Earth. After that I always wanted to be a police officer, but I got involved in gangs, got pregnant, got married, became a mother, and ended up being an abused wife. *Two Badges* is the true story of how I became a police woman.

Related Titles:

Amá, Your Story Is Mine: Walking Out of the Shadows of Abuse by Ercenia "Alice" Cedeño. University of Texas Press, 2007

91. The Unwanted: A Memoir

Author: **Kien Nguyen** was born in South Vietnam in 1967 to a Vietnamese mother and an American father. In 1985 he went to a refugee camp in the Philippines, and then to the United States. The author of novels and a memoir, he lives in Houston, Texas, where he is president of Little Saigon Radio. <www.aviv2.com/kien>

Publication: Little Brown, 2001. 343 pages

Genre: Memoir   *Level:* Adult

Note: NCM Pulitzera Award for Ethnic Writers

Subjects: Nguyen, Kien, Refugees, Vietnam War, 1961-1975, Vietnamese Americans—Biography

Read-aloud excerpt: Pages 20 through 23

Booktalk: Kien Nguyen was born in South Vietnam in 1967. His mother was Vietnamese. His father was an American engineer who left when Kien was three. His mother and her two sons lived a life of luxury until 1975 when the U.S. Army withdrew. Nguyen Van Thieu, the president of South Vietnam quit and fled the country. Kien's mother made arrangements for her family to leave South Vietnam, but her parents refused to leave. Because of the delay, the family was trapped in Saigon when the Vietcong arrived. For the next ten years Kien and his family struggled to survive under the new regime. Because he and his brother were "half breeds," Amerasian children, and because their mother had been a wealthy property owner, they endured many hardships until finally in 1985 they were allowed to leave Vietnam. This memoir is Kien Nguyen's account of how he survived the aftermath of the Vietnam War to become a citizen of the United States.

Related Titles:

Land of Smiles: A Novel by T. C. Huo. Plume, 2000

92. Wait for Me

Author: **An Na**, Korean American, grew up in California and now lives in Vermont. Her first novel *A Step from Heaven* was an award winner. *Wait for Me* is her second novel. <www.anwriting.com/author.html>

Publication: Putnam, 2006. 172 pages

Genre: Contemporary fiction   *Level:* Young Adult

Summary: As her senior year approaches, Mina yearns to find her path in life but working at the family business, taking care of her sister, and dealing with her mother's expectations are as stifling as the California heat, until she falls in love.

Subjects: California—Fiction, Hearing impaired, Korean Americans—Fiction, Mothers and daughters—Fiction, Self-actualization

Read-aloud excerpt: Page 5 through 7

Booktalk: Mina Kang tries to be the perfect daughter but that is not working out very well lately. Her younger sister Suna is troubled; sleepwalking; sometimes does not wear her hearing aid; and Mina has to be like a mother to her since their mother does not have any patience with Suna. Their mother's dream is for Mina to go to Harvard. Mina will try to get an excellent score on her SATs, but she knows that her grades are not good enough even if she does well on the tests. Because of all the pressure, things have gotten complicated for Mina. She is lying to her mother, sneaking money from their dry cleaning business, and trying to avoid Jonathan Kim, who knows what she is doing and could ruin everything if she does not do what he wants. After their dad hurts his back and Ysrael starts to work at the dry cleaners, Mina wants to get to know him better. Does she dare?

Related Titles:
A Step From Heaven by An Na. Front Street, 2001
Good Enough by Paula Yoo. HarperTeen, 2008

93. West of the Jordan

Author: **Laila Halaby** is Jordanian American, daughter of a Jordanian father and an American mother. A student of folklore, a Fulbright scholar, and published author of fiction and poetry, she lives in Arizona. <www.lailahalaby.net/about>

Publication: Beacon Press, 2003. 220 pages

Genre: Contemporary fiction   *Level:* Adult

Note: PEN Beyond Margins Award

Summary: Four Arab and Arab American cousins tell of their coming of age experiences.

Subjects: Arab Americans—Fiction, Coming of age, Domestic fiction, Jordan

Read-aloud excerpt: Pages 8 through 9

Booktalk: This is the story of three Arab American cousins with connections to the Jordanian village of Nawara. Hala was living in Arizona when her mother died. Soraya has embraced American freedom and wears makeup, speaks ghetto slang, and had an affair with a married man. Her mother cannot wait for her to graduate from high school so she can be married off without further disgracing the family. Khadija is afraid of her father, an angry man who has lost his hopes and dreams. He once forced his daughter to drink alcohol and then called her a dog and hit her again and again until she ran and hid. A fourth cousin, Mawal still lives in the village of Nawara. Many of the village women grieve because it seems their husbands and sons have gone to the U.S. and been exposed to the evils of drinking, drugs, gambling, and loose women. Mawal would like to go and see for herself what life in America is really like.

Related Titles:

Arabian Jazz by Diana Abu-Jaber. Harcourt Brace, 1993

The Girl in the Tangerine Scarf by Mohja Kahf. Carroll & Graf, 2006

Once In a Promised Land by Laila Halaby. Beacon Press, 2007

Swimming Toward the Light by Angela Tehaan Leone. Syracuse University Press, 2007

94. *When Kambia Elaine Flew in From Neptune*

Author: **Lori Aurelia Williams**, African American, was born in Houston, Texas and now lives in Austin, Texas. Williams is the author of novels for teens.

<www.teenreads.com/authors/au-williams-lori.asp>

Publication: Simon & Schuster, 2000. 246 pages

Genre: Contemporary fiction   *Level:* Young Adult

Note: Popular Paperbacks for Young Adults (ALA), AudioFile Earphones Award

Summary: Shayla Dubois learns about life when her sister Tia leaves home, her father returns, and Kambia Elaine moves in next door.

Subjects: African Americans—Fiction, Child abuse, Coming of age, Domestic fiction, Houston, Texas, Texas—Fiction

Read-aloud excerpt: Pages 3 through 5

Booktalk: The trouble started when their mother found a package of condoms in Shayla's sister Tia's dresser drawer. About that time Shayla gets acquainted with Kambia Elaine, the strange girl who has just moved in next door. Kambia wears the same dingy white dress day after day. At various times Kambia declares herself to be a piece of driftwood or a pecan tree. She is like no one Shayla has ever known. She talks about Lizard People and Wallpaper Wolves. Shayla's home life gets increasingly complicated. Tia and Mama get into a huge fight, and Tia disappears. Then Shayla's father comes to visit and after a few days moves into their house. Shayla, who wants to be a writer someday, is having trouble making sense of everything that is happening. Her grandmother has told her she should never break her word, and Shayla did promise she would not tell, but now she is not sure. Should she tell what she knows or keep her word?

Related Titles:

I Hadn't Meant to Tell You This by Jacqueline Woodson. Delacorte, 1994

95. When Thunders Spoke

Author: **Virginia Driving Hawk Sneve**, Sioux, grew up on the Rosebud Sioux Reservation in South Dakota. Author of books for children and adults, she lives in South Dakota.

<http://voices.cla.umn.edu/vg/Bios/entries/sneve_virginia_driving_hawk.html>

Publication: Holiday House, 1974. 93 pages

Genre: Contemporary fiction   *Level:* Young Adult

Note: Author was a National Humanities Medalist.

Summary: After a fifteen-year-old Sioux finds a sacred stick, unusual things begin to happen to his family.

Subjects: Dakota Indians—Fiction, Indians of North America—Fiction

Read-aloud excerpt: Pages 13 through 14

Booktalk: Norman Two Bull lives on the Dakota reservation in a shabby little house with no indoor plumbing. His grandfather, who knows the old ways and beliefs, spends his summers in a tent in the area. Norman's mother joined a church in the community and now thinks of the old ways and stories as "heathenish." Norman often climbs Thunder Butte in search of agates, which he trades at the trading post for candy for his mother. Norman wants the rifle that hangs on the wall of the trading post but knows that he cannot afford such an expensive item. He wishes for a tumbler to polish agates and sell them to tourists himself. When Norman follows the instructions of his grandfather and climbs to a different side of Thunder Butte, he finds an antique coup stick that his grandfather says is sacred. Norman takes the coup stick home and his father hangs it on the wall. His mother hates it and wants it out of her house, but his father believes that good things will happen because of the stick. Norman wishes he had never found it because of the friction between his parents. During the next days, both the coup stick and their lives seem to be changing.

Related Titles:

Indian Summers by Eric Gansworth. Michigan State University, 1998.

Smoke Dancing by Eric Gansworth. Michigan State University Press, 2004.

96. Where Do I Go From Here?

Author: **Valerie Wilson Wesley**, African American, was artist-in-residence at Columbia College, editor of *Essence* magazine, is the author of mysteries, short stories, and novels for children and adults, and lives in New Jersey. <www.tamarahayle.com/biography.html>

Publication: Scholastic, 1993. 138 pages

Genre: Contemporary fiction   *Level:* Young Adult

Note: Best Books for Reluctant Readers (ALA)

Summary: Nia and Marcus, two of the very few African American students at a snooty prep school, struggle to find out what they want to do with their lives.

Subjects: African Americans—Fiction, Boarding schools—Fiction, Schools—Fiction

Read-aloud excerpt: Pages 1 through 5

Booktalk: Nia's only real friend at Endicott Academy is Marcus Garvey Williams. Both Nia and Marcus are African American, both scholarship students at this very expensive prep school. Nia is back for her second year at Endicott, still learning to deal with the rich kids and the snobs who make up most of the student body. She stays at the school because of her Aunt Odessa who raised her after Nia's parents died when she was little. Aunt Odessa is convinced that graduating from Endicott will help Nia's future. Endicott is bearable only because of Marcus, and now something is very wrong with Marcus. He needs money and he wants Nia to meet him in McCarter's Woods in the middle of the night to give him the money. Nia wants to help, but she knows that if they are caught together, they could both be expelled. Why does he need the money? Is it worth the risk?

Related Titles:

Brother Hood by Janet McDonald. Farrar, Straus and Giroux, 2004

97. While the Locust Slept

Author: **Peter Razor**, a member of the Fond du Lac band of Ojibwa, grew up in Minnesota. Razor has researched his American Indian culture, dances in powwows, and makes traditional clothing and musical instruments using traditional methods.

Publication: Minnesota Historical Society Press, 2001. 200 pages

Genre: Memoir   *Level:* Adult

Note: Minnesota Book Award Winner

Subjects: Child abuse, Indians of North America—Biography, Minnesota State Public School, Ojibwa Indians—Biography, Razor, Peter

Read-aloud excerpt: Pages 196 through 200

Booktalk: Peter Razor is Ojibwa. Shortly after he was born, his mother and his brother Leonard, who was hydrocephalic, were placed in an asylum. Relatives took his brother Arnold to live with them, but Peter was left with his father. His father abandoned him when Peter was ten months old. He was declared a ward of the state of Minnesota and went to live at the State Public School in Owatonna. During the fifteen years he lived there, Peter and other children were often savagely beaten and abused. Many died. When Peter was fifteen, he was "placed" with a family on a farm. Previously this practice had been referred to as "indenture," but in fact it was nothing short of slavery. Orphans became a source of free labor for unscrupulous farmers. Because he had no family or friends to check on his welfare, Peter was left to the mercy of a brutal man who drank and beat his wife and the boy he had agreed to take care of. This is Peter Razor's account of how he survived the nightmare of his first seventeen years and went on to lead a successful life, raise a family, and learn about the culture of his people.

Related Titles:

Lost in the System by Charlotte Lopez and Susan Dworkin. Simon & Schuster, 1996

Stewing in the Melting Pot: The Memoir of a Real American by Robert Sanabria. Capital
   Books, 2001

98. White Girl

Author: **Sylvia Olsen** grew up in British Columbia. She married a Tsartlip First Nation man and has four children who have grown up in the Tsartlip community. Olsen writes and works with community management.
<www.stellaraward.ca/author.php?id=12>

Publication: Sononis Press, 2004. 235 pages

Genre: Contemporary fiction   *Level:* Young Adult

Note: Stellar Award, BC's Teen Readers' Choice Award

Summary: When Josie was fourteen her mother married an Indian and moved from town to the reserve where she is the outsider.

Subjects: Canada, Indians of North America—Fiction

Read-aloud excerpt: Pages 7 through 8

Booktalk: I'm Josie. I was fifteen when my forty-year-old mother came home one night with smudged lipstick and a dreamy look in her eyes. She had fallen in love with an Indian man. The next thing I knew, we were driving out to the reserve where Martin lived. Then it was just a few weeks until Mom announced that she and Martin were getting married. After she and my dad divorced, Mom always said there was no such thing as happily ever after, but obviously she changed her mind. They got married and after a short honeymoon, we loaded up our stuff in a pickup truck and moved into Martin's house. That is where I am now. Trapped. In Martin's house on the reserve. Forty minutes from civilization. No car. No friends. At least I have a room of my own. At least in here nobody calls me "Blondie" or "white girl." Then there is Luke, my new stepbrother. He's a studly hunk. I wonder what he thinks of his new white stepsister.

Related Titles:

The Girl with a Baby by Sylvia Olsen. Sono Nis Press, 2003

99. Who Am I Without Him? Short Stories about Girls and the Boys in Their Lives

Author: **Sharon G. Flake**, author of a number of award-winning books, is African American. Born in Philadelphia, she has worked as a youth counselor and in public relations. She lives in Pittsburgh. <www.sharongflake.com>

Publication: Jump at the Sun, 2004. 168 pages

Genre: Contemporary fiction (short stories)   *Level:* Young Adult

Note: Coretta Scott King Award Winner

Summary: Ten short stories about growing up African American.

Subjects: African Americans—Fiction, Dating (Social customs), Family life—Fiction

Read-aloud excerpt: Pages 29 through 31

Booktalk: *So I Ain't No Good Girl* because my man Raheem left me for a good girl, one of those straight A girls, a cheerleader, a flute player in the band, but I got him back, my sweet Raheem, even if I ain't a good girl.

The Ugly One, that's what they call me. Sometimes the girls call me Marbles because I've got these bumps all over my face. There's no cure for what I've got, and nobody sees past my ugly face.

Wanted: A Thug Why? I got a good man that's on the basketball team, has good manners, and treats me good. What's the problem? He's so nice, he's boring.

I Know a Stupid Boy When I See One so how come if I'm so smart, I'm here dying?

These and six more stories in this book are about girls and boys, men and women and how hard life is because of the differences between us. Maybe you have noticed that too?

Related Titles:

Brides and Sinners in El Chuco by Christine Granados. University of Arizona Press, 2006
Orange Candy Slices and Other Secret Tales by Viola Canales. Piñata Books, 2001
El Milagro and Other Stories by Patricia Preciado Martin. University of Arizona Press, 1996

100. X-Indian Chronicles: The Book of Mausape

Author: **Thomas Yeahpau** grew up in Anadarko, Oklahoma. A member of the Kiowa Tribe, he lives in Los Angeles. Yeahpau has worked as a screenwriter, music and film producer, and actor. He is a storyteller and a poet.

Publication: Candlewick Press, 2006. 232 pages

Genre: Contemporary fiction   *Level:* Adult

Note: Western Writers of America Spur Award Best First Novel Finalist

Summary: Interwoven stories chronicle the lives of several X-Indians, Indians who have lost their traditional beliefs, traditions, and medicines, as they become young men.

Subjects: Conduct of life, Indians of North America—Fiction

Read-aloud excerpt: Pages 3 through 5

Booktalk: Mausape along with Rodney, Marlon, and James, also known as Hoss, Brando, and Maddog, grew up in NDN City. They are X-Indians. Mausape is the poet who tells their stories. Their grandparents had traditional beliefs, medicines, and legends. Two generations later, Mausape and his friends are becoming assimilated and losing the traditions. Their world is a fantastic satirical world of violence and loneliness, alcohol and drugs, love and sex, crime and jails. These are the life stories of a group of young X-Indians and their modern-day vision quests.

Related Titles:
The Absolutely True Diary of a Part-Time Indian by Sherman Alexie. Little, Brown, 2007

101. Year in Nam: A Native American Soldier's Story

Author: **Leroy TeCube**, Jicarilla Apache, grew up in New Mexico and is a Vietnam War veteran. TeCube works in the Environmental Protection Office of the Jicarilla Apache Tribe in New Mexico. <www.ipl.org/div/natam/bin/browse.pl/A521>

Publication: University of Nebraska Press, 1999. 261 pages

Genre: Memoir   *Level:* Adult

Note: American Book Award, North American Indian Prose Award

Subjects: Indians of North America—Biography, TeCube, Leroy, 1947, Vietnam War, 1961-1975

Read-aloud excerpt: Pages xviii through xix

Booktalk: My name is Leroy TeCube. I am Jicarilla Apache. My mother died when I was about a year old so I lived with relatives until I started school. I attended a Bureau of Indian Affairs elementary school and lived in a dormitory. During high school, I spent time with my aunt and uncle and learned much about being outdoors, hunting, and Indian ways. After I finished high school, I was planning to join the Marines but got my draft notice and joined the Army instead. Like thousands of Indians who fought with other Americans in World War I, World War II, Korea, and Vietnam, I carried on the warrior tradition. For one year of my life, from January 1968, until January 1969, I was an infantryman in Vietnam. This book contains recollections of the Vietnam War from my point of view.

Related Titles:

Aztlán and Viet Nam edited by George Mariscal. University of California Press, 1999

A Patriot After All by Juan Ramirez. University of New Mexico Press, 1999

Soldados: Chicanos in Viet Nam by Charley Trujillo. Chusma House Publications, 1990

Son of Two Bloods by Vincent L. Mendoza. University of Nebraska Press, 1996

The Three Wars of Roy Benavidez by Roy P. Benavidez and Oscar Griffin. Corona Publishing Company, 1986

Resources

Billan, Maria Mazziotti and Jennifer Gillan, eds. *Growing Up Ethnic in America: Contemporary Fiction about Learning to Be American.* Penguin Books, 1999.

Cao, Lan and Himilce Novas. *Everything You Need to Know About Asian-American History.* Plume, 1996.

Cruz, Bárbara C. *Multiethnic Teens and Cultural Identity: A Hot Issue.* Enslow, 2001.

De Jesús, Joy L. ed. *Growing Up Puerto Rican: An Anthology.* Avon Books, 1997.

Fernandez-Shaw, Carlos M. *The Hispanic Presence in North America From 1492 to Today.* Rev. ed. Facts on File, 1999.

Garrod, Andrew and Robert Kilkenny, eds. *Balancing Two Worlds: Asian American College Students Tell Their Life Stories.* Cornell University Press, 2007.

Garrod, Andrew and Colleen Larimore, eds. *First Person, First Peoples: Native American College Graduates Tell Their Life Stories.* Cornell University Press, 1997.

Garrod, Andrew, Robert Kilkenny, and Christina Gómez, eds. *Mi Voz, Mi Vida: Latino College Students Tell Their Life Stories.* Cornell University Press, 2007.

Gonzalez, Juan. *Harvest of Empire: A History of Latinos in America.* Viking, 2000.

Green, Rayna and Melanie Fernandez. *The Encyclopedia of the First Peoples of North America.* Groundwood, 1999.

Nabokov, Peter, ed. *Native American Testimony: A Chronicle of Indian-White Relations from Prophecy to the Present 1492-1992.* Penguin Books, 1991.

Novas, Himilce. *Everything You Need to Know About Latino History.* Revised edition. Plume, 1998.

O'Hearn, Claudine Chiawei, ed. *Half and Half: Writers on Growing Up Biracial and Bicultural.* Pantheon Books, 1998.

Ochoa, George. *The New York Public Library Amazing Hispanic American History: A Book of Answers for Kids.* John Wiley & Sons, 1998.

Takaki, Ronald. *A Different Mirror: A History of Multicultural America.* Little, Brown, 1993.

Subject Index

Cubanita
Emily Goldberg Learns to Salsa
Girls for Breakfast
Lorenzo's Secret Mission
Plain City
Illegal aliens
Ask Me No Questions
Breaking Through
Immigrants—Fiction
Behind the Mountains
Blue Jasmine
Flight to Freedom
Fresh Off the Boat
The Treasure in the Tiny Blue Tin
India
Blue Jasmine
Naming Maya
Indians of North America—Biography
Bloodlines
Bowman's Store
Indian Boyhood
While the Locust Slept
Year in Nam
Indians of North America—Fiction
The Education of Ruby Loonfoot
Flight
Power
Rain Is Not My Indian Name
The Secret of Dead Man's Mine
When Thunders Spoke
White Girl
X-Indian Chronicles
Individuality
Beacon Hill Boys
Interpersonal relations
Behind the Eyes
Blue Jasmine
Cubanita
Emako Blue
Loves Me, Loves Me Not
Interracial dating
If You Come Softly
Mismatch
Iowa City, Iowa
Blue Jasmine
Israel
The Singing Mountain

J

Japanese Americans—Biography
Dandelion Through the Crack
Japanese Americans—Fiction
Beacon Hill Boys
Mismatch

Jaramillo, Mari-Luci
Madame Ambassador
Jerusalem
Habibi
Jewish-Arab relations
Habibi
Jews—Biography
Out of the Shadows
Jews—Fiction
Birdland
Confessions of a Closet Catholic
Double Crossing
Emily Goldberg Learns to Salsa
The Flood
Never Mind the Goldbergs
The Singing Mountain
The Treasure in the Tiny Blue Tin
Jordan
West of the Jordan
Journalists—Biography
American Chica

K

Kansas
The Flood
Korean Americans—Fiction
Finding My Hat
Finding My Voice
Girls for Breakfast
Tae's Sonata
Wait for Me

L

Law enforcement
Two Badges
Lee, William Poy, 1950-
The Eighth Promise
Loss (Psychology)
The Meaning of Consuelo

M

Mariachi (Motion picture)
Rebel Without a Crew
Mexican Americans—Biography
Always Running
Barefoot Heart
Barrio Boy
Breaking Through
Burro Genius
Hunger of Memory
Madame Ambassador
The Making of a Civil Rights Leader
Nobody's Son
Rebel Without a Crew
Two Badges

TITLE INDEX

AUTHOR INDEX

S

Sáenz, Andrés 27
Sáenz, Benjamin Alire 65
Salas, Floyd 29
Saldaña, René, Jr. 46
Sanabria, Robert 79
Sanchez, Alex 40
Sandoval, Victor M. 21
Santiago, Esmeralda 3, 4, 88
Sato, Kiyo 25
Schorr, Melissa 13
Senna, Danzy 51
Sheth, Kashmira 15
Sidhwa, Bapsi 7
Silva, Simón 18
Smith, Cynthia Leitich 63-64
Sneve, Virginia Driving Hawk 15, 77
Son, John 35
Soto, Gary 2, 8-9, 21, 44
Stavans, Ilan 43
Stork, Francisco X. 10
Suárez, Virgil 68-69

T

Takahashi, Grace 26
Takaki, Ronald 52, 83
Tal, Eve 28
Tan, Amy 67
Tarantino, Quentin 65
TeCube, Leroy 81, 89
Thomas, Piri 28, 89
Tijerina, Andrés 27
Triana, Gaby 24
Trujillo, Charley 82
Tywoniak, Frances Esquibel 9

U

Ulibarrí, Sabine R. 51, 89
Urrea, Luis Alberto 56-57, 89

V

Veciana-Suarez, Ana 37, 48
Velásquez, Gloria L. 40, 69
Villanueva, Alma Luz 72
Villanueva, Marianne 39
Villaseñor, Victor 20, 89
Viramontes, Helena María 63

W

Waldman, Neil 60, 89
Walker, Rebecca 46
Weiner, Hollace Ava 72
Wesley, Valerie Wilson 78
Williams, Lori Aurelia 76
Wilson, Gilbert L. 45
Wolff, Ferida 22
Wong, Joyce Lee 66
Wong, Shawn 5
Wood, Frances M. 26
Woods, Brenda 31
Woodson, Jacqueline 43-44, 76

Y

Yamanaka, Lois-Ann 53
Yang, Gene 5
Yeahpau, Thomas M. 81
Yee, Lisa 27
Yep, Laurence 27
Yoo, David 41
Yoo, Paula 75